2 work

Lightning
Less

OPERATION ELVIS

Operation Elvis

Alan Levy

illustrated by Dedini

ANDRE DEUTSCH

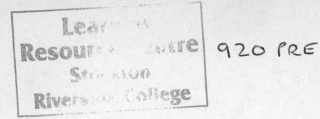
First Published 1960 by
André Deutsch Limited
12–14 Carlisle Street Soho Square
London W1
© Alan Levy 1960
Printed in Great Britain by
Photolithography at
The Curwen Press
Plaistow E13

Contents

to Val

"Only the perfect man can go about
in the modern world without attracting
attention to himself."

—Chuangtse, Chinese philosopher, *circa* 300 B.C.

1

"I Got a Little Break Outta Life"

*"Please, please, please don't draft Elvis Presley! . . .
not only for his or my welfare, but for the Army's as
well . . . Letters will jam up the mailing system
. . . the WACs will start riots wherever he shows
up . . . The Army will never be the same."*

—letter from a 15-year-old Honolulu girl, to Memphis military officials.

On March 24, 1958, the United States Army undertook a mission as complex as a wartime invasion, as precarious as the second stripe on a corporal's sleeve.

Objective: to transform a $105,000-a-month rock-'n'-roll idol into an $83.20-a-month GI . . . to convert one civilian—nomenclature: Mr. Elvis "The Pelvis" Presley—into Army private US53310761 . . . and to treat him "just like everyone else" throughout his two-year hitch.

3

Operation Elvis was conducted before a grandstand many times larger than all the armories, auditoriums, stadiums, and theaters Elvis Presley had ever packed. Teenagers, who had worked the first miracle of transforming a Memphis truck-driver into a world-famous millionaire, watched to see if the Army could reverse their handiwork. Each teenager felt at least a particle of involvement—positive or negative—with Elvis. Servicemen and draft-board members couldn't resist a sense of identification, since the systems for which they worked so thanklessly were under scrutiny, and morale was at stake. Youths whose "military obligation" loomed ahead wondered how they would fare at the same crossroads. Veterans who had completed their hitches years or months earlier peered through clouds of confusion in an effort to discern "The Old Army" or "The New Army" or "Elvis Presley's Army" in action. From behind its usual sincere show of patriotism, the entertainment world gazed apprehensively, wondering if Elvis might emerge from his two years in the Army as a popularity "casualty," missing from the action of a fickle public. Others hinted that trading in Elvis' blue suede shoes for size-12 combat boots might be the ideal survival "gimmick" for a fad that already had outlasted its life expectancy. The press didn't need any invitation; it smelled good copy.

This was the gallery the Army could have expected when making seating arrangements.

Soon the performers began to arrive. Chambers of Commerce, Senators, and Congressmen crowded toward the center of the arena, all of them offering advice. Publicity-hounds, do-gooders, and free-lancers spilled onto the field. Women—who had nursed the Elvis rage past its most optimistic life expectancy—insisted on getting into the act. And when Operation Elvis expanded in scope, the cast was swelled by Fräuleins on both sides of the Elbe, by Russians, and by State Department brass.

The Army scanned the terrain and discovered itself in a state of siege. Hewing to the line of treating Presley "just like everyone else," it had been outflanked by "just about everyone else." And everyone else had a few suggestions, a salvo of complaints, a barrage of questions, a smoke-screen of threats, or a "foolproof" plan . . .

How well did the Army handle Elvis Presley? What did the active duty of US53310761 reveal about the Army? About the Pelvis? About the public? Is one democracy sturdy enough to support a two-year marriage of the Selective Service system to the celebrity system? Was this unlikely union good for Elvis, for service morale, for international good will, for anything but public laughs? Could Elvis and Uncle Sam part as good friends? How did his treatment compare to that received—or undergone or avoided—by other Very Important Persons when they donned the uniform? What lessons were learned? How much did it cost Elvis, the taxpayers, the tax collectors?

And just WHO was Elvis Presley to rate this 21-gun furor, anyway?

Operation Elvis started long before the public and the Army knew or cared about Elvis Aron Presley, his ducktail haircut, or his ornate sideburns. In early 1953, shortly after his 18th birthday, a Memphis boy registered for the draft, as required by law. It was a routine, insignificant event that nobody remembers much about. Elvis Presley was just a youth who lived in a public housing project and worked at any job he could find to keep his family moving along its low-income treadmill. At the time and at his age, the Army represented an adventurous, perhaps pleasant, form of security.

Within two years, Elvis Presley's views on the Army were front-page copy. He regarded the draft passively, but not ominously. He discussed it in the same terms used by most American youths. "When they call me, I'll be ready," he told an interviewer.

The press was ready long before Elvis or the Army. In 1956, *Billboard*, the amusement trade weekly, printed its own "exclusive" induction notice. According to *Billboard*, Elvis would be inducted in December at Fort Dix, N.J. According to *Bill-board*, top Army brass were meeting specially to map battle plans that would give Presley a shortened basic training period followed by an entertainment assignment and extensive dental and gum work. Assuming the Army's crack periodontal troops could salvage Elvis, he would then be allowed an early six-week furlough to make a movie. He would also be permitted to make television appearances and recordings. According to *Bill-board*, all this would be accomplished under top secrecy!

This last detail certainly was confirmed by Elvis' draft board in Memphis. "It's real funny that everybody seems to know that he's going and we don't," said one of the three members, who added matter of factly: "It is not possible for anyone to know except this board when he is called." The top secrecy of the event was emphasized when December passed without Elvis or the Army acting out *Billboard's* well-read "exclusive."

Elvis Presley would look in a mirror each day and see himself still wearing civilian clothes. Uncle Sam seemed no closer than the nearest recruiting poster—wherever that was! If Elvis had been given the time or privacy to look for posters on the street, he would have been almost as likely to find one plugging himself as one about Uncle Sam.

The two strangers were drawn together when Presley was summoned for a pre-induction physical examination in January, 1957, shortly before his 22nd birthday. To keep the summons secret, the draft board by-passed its standard mail procedure. Instead, someone who knew Presley's unlisted phone number (a friend of a friend of a friend of the board's chief clerk) made contact and told Elvis to pick up the summons from the board chairman.

Although physicals are given to batches of 40 or 50 men at the Kennedy Veterans Hospital examining station in Memphis, Elvis was enough of a VIP to rate an all-by-himself physical on an offday. Even so, advance word was "leaked," resulting in the demotion of one Memphis soldier. Inquiries about the solitary physical were answered by the chief of the

examining station: "We were alerted. Things can get a bit confused when a celebrity is called for one of these examinations."

Right on time, a white Cadillac unloaded Elvis Presley at the examining station. He wore black slacks connected to a black shirt by a black waistband; black shoes, and a crimson windbreaker trimmed in black. He was greeted by photographers, television cameramen, reporters, fans, and an Army public-relations sergeant who handed Presley a gold coin marked "Good For One Army Career." There were squeals from the hospital's inner offices and wards as women employees left their duties momentarily to gawk. A brawny sergeant was assigned to block off the hallway entrance, but a male shout of "See you in Japan, Elvis!" penetrated this barrier.

With Elvis was Dotty Harmony, a blonde Las Vegas dancer who was visiting him. She remained in the Cadillac. Photographers asked Elvis to pose with Dotty, but he replied: "No, sir, I'd rather not. She has nothing to do with this." While Dotty waited, however, she did describe Elvis to the press as "a fine physical specimen."

"It wasn't so bad," Elvis said as he left the examining station and headed for the airport, where he put Dotty on a flight to Los Angeles before he boarded another plane for New York.

The next day, Capt. Elwyn "Rip" Rowan, Memphis recruiting commander, announced that Elvis had passed gaudily and was now 1-A (available for immediate service). His mental test scores had been about average.

Within a matter of hours, the Army was involved in the worst haircut crisis since Operation Samson. Military officials in Washington, Memphis, and elsewhere received pleas not to destroy Elvis' lavish locks when they took him in. An Army spokesman in Memphis made the mistake of assuring Presley fans that Elvis would probably be assigned as an entertainer for Army Special Services, where his long hair would remain unmolested.

A New Jersey woman read this and fired off an indignant letter to Republican Senator Clifford Case:

The idea! The Army takes very intelligent young men and pushes them through the mill, usually without much regard for talents (not the hound-dog type) or intelligence. That's fine if— and I mean *if*—everyone is given the same treatment. Now I see this is not so.

Senator Case sent an inquiry to Army Secretary Wilber Brucker, who tossed it to Brigadier General J.E. Bastion, Jr., who dutifully read up on the matter and reported back: No special treatment had been promised Elvis. Bastion added, "I have been further advised that if Elvis Presley is inducted into the Army, he will receive his basic training at Fort Chaffee, Ark., in company with other draftees inducted at the same time." Whatever happened to their hair and sideburns would also happen to Elvis Presley's.

At Fort Chaffee, Capt. John Mawn, the public-information officer, thought he was re-stating the Pentagon's position when he told a reporter: "No one gets preferential treatment at Chaffee. Recruits get military haircuts the day they arrive." Asked to elaborate, Mawn described a military haircut as "the peeled-onion style."

An imaginative wire-service artist painted a peeled-onion haircut on an action photo of Elvis Presley. The resulting anguish could not have been greater if Captain Mawn had advocated germ warfare. Letters poured in to the Arkansas captain:

Dear Sir: Elvis' hair might not seem very important to you, but it is to me and a couple million other girls I know. So help me George, if you cut off Elvis' hair, I'll walk clear down to Arkansas and not only will I cut off your hair, but I'll take your whole head off with it.

Dear Captain Mawn: Please don't cut his hair. Can't you understand his hair is his trademark? How would you like for someone to cut off your trademark in a few minutes?

And, from an International Fan Club:

He would still be cute even if you scalped him. He probably has a better shaped head than all the guys in the whole damn Army.

A letter from Watertown, S.D., complained that the haircut would make Elvis resemble a "neurotic jailbird" more than a peeled onion. Petitions from Memphis and Calvert, Texas, asked the Army to retain Presley's sideburns.

More practical writers were resigned, but hopeful. Dozens requested locks of Elvis' hair. Appropriately enough, one came from Lockport, N.Y.: "If you are a Christian, or better a Catholic, you will appreciate this. I will remember you in my every prayer and Mass until I depart from this world." Radio station KLOU in Lake Charles, La., offered to auction off Elvis' hair to benefit the March of Dimes. A Hayward, Cal., boy addressed his personal request to "Sergeant Waiting For Elvis." It said, "Please send me some dust off Elvis Presley's combat boots."

Not all the letters were from cranks or dullards. A sizable fraction came from literate, intelligent people. A letter from a 15-year-old girl in Brunswick, Ga., was addressed to "Commanding Officer, Fort Chaffee." It began politely: "Dear Sir: I would like to apologize for the rather impersonal address on this envelope. I do not know your name." It ended with a fervent but dignified plea for a lock of Elvis' hair. "A stamped, self-addressed envelope is enclosed."

In March, 1957, Metro-Goldwyn-Mayer beat the Army to the shears by giving Elvis a semi-peeled onion haircut for the film, *Jailhouse Rock*. By this time, the latest rumor was that Elvis would seek a recruiting job when drafted. Elvis was interviewed on the movie set:

"I'm not worried about my hair or sideburns or what the Army's gonna do with me. Everybody who goes into the service gets their hair cut. I expect it—and I wouldn't have it any other way. I'm just a normal, healthy guy like all the rest. Only thing is, I got a little break outta life.

"Whatever the Army people want me to do is fine. I don't expect any special privileges or favors. Those people in the service are fair. They demand discipline and respect. And that's what I'll give 'em.

Hearst writer called Fort Chaffee and spoke to an Information Office major. This partial transcript was recorded by the Army:

Q: How about the haircut?

A: He will be treated just like any other young man coming into the army.

Q: What does that mean? Do the sideburns and long hair stay or go?

A: He will receive the short haircut. It is not a shaved head thing, by the way, but more of a crew cut business. The hair is more than an inch long.

Q: How about singing training?

A: We don't teach singing at Fort Chaffee.

Q: Won't it be the other way around? Presley will do the teaching.

A: If he is to teach singing, he won't be sent to Fort Chaffee.

Q: Will he be allowed to bring his guitar?

A: Yes.

The reporter attributed the interview to "a platoon sergeant." The major reportedly was neither rank-conscious nor offended; just filled with relief.

The most unenthusiastic response to Elvis' induction notice emanated from Y. Frank Freeman, head of Paramount Pictures. Filming of *King Creole*, starring Elvis Presley, was scheduled to start January 13. If the film had to be canceled, it would mean a $350,000 loss for the California studio.

Freeman, hoping to salvage Paramount's investment without impairing national security, asked the Memphis board for an eight-week delay of Elvis' induction. This was not an unusual request. It is generally granted to a farmer who needs a hand a few weeks longer in the harvest season or a store that needs all the help it can keep for the Christmas rush or any business with a temporary problem.

The draft board replied that a deferment request would have to come from Elvis too.

Elvis complied. On December 24, he wrote a friendly letter to the board, explaining that he was acting not in his own interest, but on behalf of Paramount "so these folks will not lose

so much money, with everything they have done so far." He
ended the letter by wishing the three board members a Merry
Christmas.

Three days later, the board wished Mr. Presley and Paramount a happy, prosperous New Year by unanimously grant-
ing the request and deferring Elvis until March 24. To the
board members, it was a semi-routine decision.

2

"You Didn't Put Beethoven in the Army"

"I think it's a shame to take such good talent away from the American public. I can't act or sing like Elvis can, but I can serve in the Army as well as he, so I want you to take me in his place and let him go . . ."

—letter from 18-year-old Kalamazoo boy to Fort Chaffee.

Instead of jingle bells, a jangling telephone caroled in the holiday season at the Memphis home of Milton Bowers, Sr. As chairman of Local Board 86, Bowers was the man who both drafted and deferred Elvis within a week. He became a hero to some, a villain to others, a target for crackpot calls, and a temporary insomniac. People felt free to phone Bowers at any hour—a few to tell him he was "the greatest"; many to inform him he was the least.

"You didn't put Beethoven in the Army, did you?" said **one** midnight caller who was convinced that Bowers discriminated against rock-'n'-roll music.

"Well, sir, considering that Beethoven wasn't an American and has been dead for some time and would have been 4-F for ear trouble anyway, I suppose we couldn't have done much with him," Bowers replied evenly. "After all, sir, we put Mr. Eisenhower in the Army and that ought to count for something."

Many calls and letters were so thickly coated with verbal vitriol that it was impossible to determine which side the complainer was on. Pro-Presley people objected to the idea of inducting their hero; anti-Elvisites objected to the deferment.

Bowers—a wiry, active man in his early sixties—had expected the worst, but the abuse he received surpassed his most lurid nightmares:

"One woman said she hoped my wife and all my children died. 'I wish you all the bad luck in the world,' that's what she said."

Such sentiments had been unknown to a gentle soul like Bowers, who makes a point of kissing both his grown, married sons good night when they go home from the family welding company.

"I got one letter from a woman who said that if we drafted Elvis, she was coming down here to kill the whole damn board," he said. "Can you imagine that? I turned her letter over to the police."

A few days after the deferment, Bowers reported; "I'm fed to the teeth. I eat, sleep, and drink Elvis Presley. In fact, I talk Elvis Presley more than I sleep. I must have talked a thousand dollars' worth of long-distance calls on the boy. With all due respect to Elvis, who's a nice boy, we've drafted people who are far, far more important than he is. After all, when you take him out of the entertainment business, what have you got left? A truck driver!"

Bowers, a former Democratic State Legislator and onetime president of the Memphis school board, had one consolation: "I got some wires and a lot of support from sound-thinking, clean-minded people, but they're not usually the kind who write letters. My mail was mostly Anti."

Among the prominent "Anti's" was State Representative H. Nick Johnson of Harlan, Ky., several hundred miles northeast of Memphis. Johnson, a 37-year-old Purple Heart veteran of World War II, resigned from his draft board when he read that Elvis had been granted a deferment to finish a movie. "It made it impossible for me to serve as a member of Local Board 35," he wrote, adding that if finishing a movie "is a criterion for deferment, then the sputnik and muttnik age isn't as serious as represented. I cannot conscientiously ask any mountain boy to serve the same country unless afforded the same treatment as Presley."

Johnson didn't need a Geiger counter to learn that his devious logic had struck a rich vein in his mining town. Ike Massey, a Harlan cab driver, shook hands with Johnson and burst into tears. "I'm for you. I lost a son in World War II," Massey wailed. County Judge Cam Smith, whose son was killed in Europe ten days before World War II ended, said: "If my son had a sixty-day deferment, he'd be with me today." To many of Johnson's constituents, evaluating the issue was as easy as putting a dime in a jukebox. Harlan coal miners simply argued the case on the merits of Elvis Presley's style. Elvis sings the kind of music they "dig," although many of the miners don't dig it the way Elvis sings it.

Johnson's resignation made him a national hero-for-a-day when the Associated Press publicized his outburst. Scores of newspapers carried the story and his picture throughout the United States. A few weary draft-board members seized the occasion as an excuse to exit with fanfare from an unpaid, after-hours, and mostly thankless voluntary post.

Despite his new leisure, Johnson was kept as busy as Milton Bowers. He answered four hundred calls, many of them long distance, and opened hundreds of letters. A teenage girl informed him: "You shouldn't talk about Elvis like that. You should be strung up."

But the dark-haired State legislator reported that the communications he received ran about 16 to 1 in support of his stand. A woman called long distance to urge that "we march on Washington to end draft discrimination." Johnson was most flattered by an ex-GI who operated an Indiana gas station. The Hoosier phoned for a picture of Johnson to be hung in the service station's office. He also wanted Johnson "to introduce a bill in Congress" abolishing the draft. Johnson explained to his dedicated admirer that a State Representative does not introduce Congressional legislation.

Johnson's constituents kept his story alive by sending wires and letters in all directions. American Legion Post 54 in Harlan wrote Bowers that "preferred treatment of this sort is detrimental to the draft boards of America and to the morale of service- and ex-servicemen." The commander of a nearby Veterans of Foreign Wars post added that "draft deferments should not be made to anyone except in cases of extreme hardship." And the Harlan Chamber of Commerce gave its local boy a boost when President James Brooks sent to Selective Service Director Lewis Hershey a telegram protesting "preferential treatment."

In Washington, Hershey answered all complaints by noting that Selective Service delegates authority to local draft boards. He said the case would be left to the Memphis board "unless someone makes an appeal who has the right to appeal."

Given added fuel by the approaching expiration of the Selective Service Act and mounting debate over its renewal, the discussion staggered on. A Cincinnati *Times-Star* survey showed Elvis' deferment decidedly unpopular. The prevailing opinion was represented by a 17-year-old high school senior's frugal oversimplification, "He's no different from anybody else."

The deferment explosion and the early haircut skirmishes made it clear that Operation Elvis would never have the smoothness of a Guy Lombardo medley. It had already taken on an uncontrollable rock-'n'-roll frenzy. Navy recruiters— jumping in with appealing pitches to Elvis, the public, and anybody who'd listen—conducted themselves like blue-suited advertising agency men wondering too late how the boys over at Hup, Two, Three & Four, Inc., had snared the big account.

Newsmen tried to keep the controversy throbbing by exhuming the military histories of Joe Louis and several regiments of World War II celebrities, many of whom had earned their ribbons in Special Services, the Army's entertainment branch. The articles noted that draftees Vic Damone and Eddie Fisher had been assigned to entertain the troops during the Korean conflict. Damone, in fact, had been specifically entrusted with the mission of recruiting women for military service. One of his major Army duties was to popularize a song called "The Girls Are Marching."

The hazards of making a musical hero stand reveille never were more incisively illustrated than in 1951, when accordionist Dick Contino received his "Greeting." Contino, a more wholesome-seeming type than Elvis Presley, was described by a Hollywood columnist as a youth who "doesn't drink, doesn't smoke, takes his mother along on tours, turns over his paycheck to his father, doesn't swear or tell dirty jokes in front of ladies . . . wishes he knew more girls like his sister . . . and smiles as pretty as anyone since Valentino."

Still smiling prettily, Contino took his mother and father along for his induction at Fort Ord, Cal. They arrived several days in advance. When Contino's name was called for the induction ceremony, his parents were still at Fort Ord but the 20-year-old accordionist was not. He had disappeared.

Five days later, Contino—accompanied by his mother, doctor, lawyer, priest, and press agent—turned himself in to federal authorities. He pleaded "panic claustrophobia" and said, "I just got confused and walked out . . . I couldn't stand to be in an enclosure. Everything at Fort Ord was behind a fence and it just made me sick all over."

Before Contino saw the fences of Fort Ord again, he spent four months contemplating the walls of a federal prison. He was redrafted in 1952 and sent to Korea, where he made sergeant in his two years—a difficult accomplishment for any draftee.

Army officers turned as green as their new uniforms whenever they anticipated another Contino crisis. Early in 1958, officers at Fort Chaffee abandoned their coffee breaks to plan Elvis Presley's initial processing and basic training. They drew up schedules to cover Zero-Hour-Minus and Zero-Hour-Plus. They relieved eight Public Information Office men of their extra military duties and alerted them to work on a 24-hour-a-day basis when Presley arrived. The staff was bolstered temporarily by an extra information officer from the New Mexico Military District. The Pentagon, called upon for advice, simply urged caution: "Make as few statements as possible and keep them dignified."

Fort Chaffee's policy-makers, heeding the word from Washington, responded with a set of elaborate ground rules: "No female partners allowed in photo coverage. . . . The possibility of fan clubs, local or otherwise, attempting to 'crash in' should be considered. Public announcement should be made to the effect that such organizations and/or individuals are strictly off limits."

In the Presley camp, too, there were long strategy meetings. The double objective was to give Elvis the best financial break during his two-year hiatus and to keep the Elvis Image fresh in the public mind.

The financial outlook boiled down to a $104,916.80 loss of income for each month Elvis was not a civilian. This was based on his minimum annual take from two movies and a dozen personal appearances.

Elvis' absence from the big-money market would also cost Uncle Sam more than $500,000 a year in taxes that would have been collected from Presley.

Despite this, Elvis Presley would remain a blue-chip corporation. In addition to his private's salary of $83.20-a-month, he would receive a percentage of the gross from four earlier movies, a base salary of $1,000-a-week from RCA-Victor, record royalties, plus receipts from his own music-publishing firm and various Elvis Presley novelties. If Elvis could make more recordings while on pass or furlough (thirty days of leave time a year), his 1958 income would reach the six-figure bracket.

While his brain trust pondered his fiscal future, Elvis went about his business. On the set of King Creole a month before induction, Elvis was calm about his impending Army career. "I'm looking forward to going in," he confided to a syndicated Hollywood columnist. "I think it'll be a great experience."

He was asked if he thought a tough sergeant or two might try to give the famous Elvis Presley a hard time.

"Well, if they do, it won't be because of anything I do to provoke it. I'm goin' in to be a soldier and the Army can do anything it wants with me and send me anyplace."

Here was a philosophical attitude that could be recommended to any youth of draft age and to the clamorous public.

Before returning to Memphis for a nine-day "last fling," Elvis was given a pre-induction Hollywood send-off at which he received a Civil War musket and ate part of a cake topped by a figure of an Army private peeling potatoes.

In Memphis, Presley had to buy his civilian privacy. He rented a rollerskating rink for eight nights at $65-a-night to in-

dulge in his favorite recreation. He would show up some time
after the rink officially closed at 10:30 P.M.

No fewer than twelve beautiful girls were in and out of his
mansion as house guests that week. He also dated some Memphis belles. On his last Saturday night as a civilian, Elvis went
rollerskating and remarked: "I'd be crazy to get married now.
I like to play the field." This was a laundered reiteration of his
famous earthy statement on the same subject: 'Why buy a cow
when you can get milk through the fence?"

On Monday, March 24—a cold, rainy day that belied the recent arrival of spring—Elvis Presley reported to Local Board
86 at 6:35 A.M., almost a half-hour early. He was accompanied
by Judy Spreckles, a blonde ex-wife of a sugar magnate, and
Lamar Fike, a 270-pound Presley crony. Fike tried to enlist
with Elvis, but he was rejected instantly as overweight. Judy
told reporters she was not Elvis' girl friend, but his best friend.
"I'm like a sister to him," she said. "Girls come and go, but
sisters stay forever."

Waiting at the draft board were Chairman Bowers, members of the Memphis and visiting press (including the London
Daily Mirror), and Presley's manager, who handed out balloons
that advertised Elvis in King Creole.

"If I seem nervous, it's because I am," Presley assured the
press. He said he wasn't dreading the next day's haircut so
much as the induction day mental test. "The simplest arith-
metic problem throws me off," Elvis reported worriedly. His
philosophy, however, was intact. "I haven't talked to anybody
about what I'll do in the Army," he said. "I'll do what they
ask." He added with apparent awe. "Those fellows are getting
up about the time I usually go to bed."

At 7:14 A.M., a bus took Presley to the Kennedy Hospital induction station, where he stripped to his shorts and underwent
blood-pressure and other tests. The press was given free rein by
the hospital, although some firm lines were drawn when a
photographer made a half-hearted try for a nude photo of the

embarrassed Elvis. Such a photo might have made the photographer a bootleg millionaire.

As the day of check-ups and processing wore on, some of Elvis' relatives, fans, and girl friends arose and crowded into the hospital area. Presley ate a box lunch and took a nap in front of a television set in the station's recreation room. He signed a loyalty certificate and sweated beads over the mental test, which he eventually passed.

A telegram from Tennessee's music-loving Governor Frank Clement told Elvis: "YOU HAVE SHOWN THAT YOU ARE AN AMERICAN CITIZEN FIRST, A TENNESSEE VOLUNTEER, AND A YOUNG MAN WILLING TO SERVE HIS COUNTRY WHEN CALLED UPON TO DO SO."

When Elvis was designated US53310761 and took the significant "one step forward," the wire services rushed to flash the first bulletins to the whole world. Less frantically, the induction station notified Fort Chaffee.

Private Presley was appointed private-in-charge of the day's quota of fourteen inductees. Both his parents were sobbing, but US53310761 was cheerful as he boarded a bus for Fort Chaffee at 5 P.M.

The chartered Greyhound rolled across the Memphis-Arkansas Bridge and halted fifteen minutes later at a West Memphis, Ark., restaurant called The Coffee Cup. The Army had hoped to avoid a mob scene by feeding the men on the Arkansas side of the Mississippi River, but it had not reckoned on Elvis' drawing power.

While Presley consumed spaghetti, salad, crackers, and two Cokes, a crowd assembled. The celebrated recruit made a dash for the bus through the service entrance. Police tried to hold the mob back, but eager girls and women tore at Presley's civilian clothes, confiscated his pen, and crushed him against the closed door of the bus.

A few harrowing minutes later, the door was opened and Private Elvis Presley was evacuated.

3

"You Bring a Lump to My Billfold"

". . . Up stepped a man
With a big cigar,
He said: 'C'mere, cat!
I'm gonna make you a star! . . .'
So I picked my guitar
With a great big grin
And the money just kept on pourin' in . . ."

—from a 1959 hit song, "The All-American Boy"

The silvery bus shook and rattled out of West Memphis and then rolled through Arkansas cotton country, a monotonous scene of distant pines and unpainted cypress shacks separated from the road by mud flats. The roads were deserted in this part of the world, where it is hard for a bus passenger to tell whether darkness is falling or the bleakness of the landscape is overpowering him.

In the early evening, the weary passengers made few attempts at conversation. An occasional, "Well, we're in the Army now," led directly to a "Yup" or a comparable conversational dead end. One draftee told another, "Well, daddy-o, only 729 more days of this crap," which provoked a five-minute argument about how many days comprise a two-year hitch and whether the men would have to serve the extra day in leap-year 1960. A few amateurs tried to sing, with occasional harmony shattered by bumps in the road. Eventually, almost everyone except the driver dozed off.

US53310761 was the quietest of the bus' quiet crew. He made no effort to count the days ahead, for he knew that time creeps like a soggy ballad when you measure it. He permitted his thoughts to dwell in the past—a few weeks, a few months back—on another kind of shake, rattle, and roll: the throbbing excitement of a typical Elvis Presley "In-Person-The-One-&-Only" show.

It started with a tap dancer, a hymn-singing quartet, and an Irish tenor, all of whom strutted and sang with detached gaiety. Each performer glanced back over his shoulder, as if some impatient backstage manager stood ready to yank him into the wings. The audience of 8,500 teenagers and a few adults rudely ignored the half-struggling mediocrity on stage and shouted their ecstasy past the performers. As the tenor climbed breathlessly to a high note, his tremulous triumph was muffled by a murmur that spread like midsummer laziness through the restless Southern armory where the first of two Elvis Presley shows had been under way for more than an hour.

"He's here," said thousands of voices. Thousands of female legs—bobby-soxed, sheer-stockinged, Elvis-gartered, Elvis-braceleted, lipsticked, occasionally Elvis-tattooed, or bare—uncoiled and thousands of necks craned awkwardly, but there was nothing to be seen except other necks bobbing in the auditorium, cigarette smoke and hot breath hanging in the stale air, and, if you looked very carefully, the Irish tenor plunging on bravely but inaudibly. Everyone knew that one of Elvis' white Cadillacs had glided up to the stage door. This was almost what everybody had been waiting for!

But they had to wait another half-hour, barely held in check by one hundred ushers, sixty policemen, and strong ropes that prevented most spectators from leaving their seats during the matinée.

Finally the stage darkened. A spotlight picked out a solitary figure onstage—but it still was not Elvis!

It was a thin young boy clad completely in black except for a pure white tie upon his tormented, twitching chest. The master of ceremonies explained that this boy had known the late James Dean! There was applause, a moment of reverent silence, and then shouting, whistling, and more applause. The boy fled the stage, apparently unconsoled by having received the biggest hand thus far.

The Elvis management presented plaques to several local disc jockeys for their extensive promotion of the singer and their encouragement of regional fan clubs. The city's Presley-pluggingest disc jockey was awarded the greatest honor of his career—the privilege of introducing Elvis to this lather of sweating girlflesh.

The introduction began with a denunciation of critics but spun its way to loftier heights: "In America, it's not the cultural commissars, not the social snobs, who have the say in choosing stars, but We The People! God bless America and God bless Elvis!"

A girl swung her purse wildly at an usher who was trying to hold her back. She missed and hit a policeman instead. All around her, a stamping chant of "We want Elvis!" dissolved into delirious squeals and exploding flashbulbs as torrents of emotion were unleashed. The whole armory was like the inside of a heavily-pounded drum.

On stage stood Elvis—the idol of every red-blooded American girl!

He wore a sharply-cut gold-leaf suit (cost: $4,000) and golden slippers (cost: $100). The glitter seemed to highlight his thick brown hair, which twirled high above his forehead in a passionate wave and descended in the ducktail style he had made

C

famous. His equally notorious sideburns and heavy-lidded eyes
were recognizable from the most distant seat in the packed
house.

The squeals became moans, the "eeeeeehs!" became "oo-
oooohs!" and the armory became relatively silent—quiet
enough for Elvis to shout "Thank you!", thump the plain guitar
strapped to his chest, and plunge into "Heartbreak Hotel," the
song that had been his first nationally successful recording. His
singing appeared whole-hearted, his guitar-strumming half-
hearted. But once Elvis had wailed the first few bars, no
sounder judgment could be made; the audience's shrieks did
not subside until the song was ended.

"Thank you!" Elvis quipped again. "You bring a lump to
my billfold." It had been widely publicized that he was getting $30,000 for the two-show stand.

He sang "Long Tall Sally" with the swivel-hipped gyrations
which had provoked an advance warning from the local police
chief that no "obscene movements" would be tolerated. Elvis
had agreed to confine his motion to forward-and-backward
movement rather than side-to-side, but every now and then
body emotion won control and his hips swung sensuously.
Each time he broke the ground rules, the audience cheered.
Elvis sang in a clean voice with sure rhythm and occasional
tenderness. As he never tried to outshout his fans, only frag-
ments of each song could be heard.

Still, the eloquent drama of his inaudible singing was worth
watching. He stood like a panther about to pounce until he
reached the heart of a song. Then he held his microphone with
the sureness and easy strength of a javelin thrower. Singing
"Don't Be Cruel" ("I don't want no uhh-thuh luuv; Bay-er-bee
it's just yew aaahhm thinkin' uuv . . ."), he knifed the air
with the mike. "Love Me Tender," the title song of his first
movie, was sung in a sinking, choking voice. A hymn was rendered with exaggerated reverence and dedicated to his grand-
parents, who spell the name the way it is pronounced—"Press-
ley."

After twenty minutes, Elvis suddenly pointed an accusing finger at the audience and bellowed: "You ain't nothin' but a hound dog!"

Nobody was insulted. Everybody stood up, for if this was not yet the national anthem, it certainly was Elvis' most sacred song. Social historians may be inclined to note that 1956 was the year President Eisenhower was re-elected, the year of the Suez Canal debacle, and the ascension year of the hound dog. Elvis' voice lost any hoarseness it might have shown earlier and, after the first few minutes of cheering, the audience subsided limply while its idol bayed his memorable melody.

Then he was gone with what one critic described as "mystic swiftness" and another termed "an exit style more like a rabbit than a hound dog."

Platoons of girls shriekingly seized the microphone he had used. Others rubbed their well-scrubbed hands in the stage dirt Elvis had trod and then kissed their palms clean. A girl offered a policeman a $100 reward if he would capture a button from Elvis' coat. Three men were arrested for drunkenness, and two girls, who had hitch-hiked several hundred miles to sneak into the armory, were held for vagrancy.

More sensible Presley fans hurried home for supper and maybe a change of clothes and a few phone calls. They had only three hours in which to get back to the armory for the evening performance—same show, same songs, same Elvis!

This picture of hysteria was not an isolated incident or merely a local explosion. From 1956 on, Elvis was a news event, a social crisis, a censorship controversy, a frequent scapegoat, and occasionally the focal point of a tragedy. In all parts of the country—in places of which he had never heard and in which he would never set foot—and in many parts of the world, people were worrying about Elvis.

Radio station WAIT in Chicago aired a 12-hour "Elvis Festival" one day. It played 133 Presley records. The station received many times that number of calls, including one from a woman who inquired when the next newscast would be. She wanted to hang out her wash, but didn't want to miss a single song. Another woman told WAIT she had canceled her dental appointment in order to hear all of Elvis. In its account of the reactions, the Associated Press reported that Chicago mothers had no trouble getting their teenagers up for school but had real trouble getting them out.

Teenage Elvis fans who did get out for school occasionally had to return home early. In Romeo, Mich., Robert Phernetton, a 16-year-old high-school student, was expelled for refusing to sacrifice his upswept, side-swirled Elvis hairdo. In Portland, Ore., Principal Leon P. Minear of Benson High School told his 1,700 male students that they had three weeks to get rid of their Elvis sideburns, ducktails, and fancy clothes. The noncompliance penalty was expulsion.

School officials in Ottawa asked the parents of eight girl students at Notre Dame Convent to withdraw their daughters from classes because the girls had disobeyed a school edict to stay away from Élvis shows in the Canadian capital.

Other girls with Presley problems took them to their source. Missing Persons Bureaus wouldn't accept reports of runaways without inquiring: "Have you checked Memphis?" Among the fifty Memphis-bound runaways recovered by police was an 18-year-old Kansas City bride who cashed her husband's allotment check to pay for her journey.

An Elvis rumor was enough to shatter "Hospital Quiet" in Jersey City, where Christ's Hospital was invaded by four hundred shouting teenagers. They had "learned" that Elvis might visit a patient. Police, using loudspeakers, restored peace. A more spectacular riot was staged in Honolulu, where four thousand teenagers rocked the dock when Elvis arrived on the liner Matsonia for two shows. In Fort Worth, a group of 16-year-old girls put their lasting affection on public record by carving "ELVIS" into their forearms with jack-knives.

Not all teenagers were pro-Presley, however. Martin Ritchie, a 14-year-old Chicago boy, joined five companions in an effort to hang Elvis in effigy. They made a dummy from old rags and newspapers, used a five-gallon can for its head, and marked it "ELVIS." They put a rope around its head and tried to hang it from a lamp post. Martin climbed the pole with the rope in his hands. He touched the light shade, stiffened, slid halfway down, and fell to the ground. Five thousand volts had passed through the boy's body. He died soon after in Holy Cross Hospital.

An anti-Elvis teenage girl lost her life in Redwood City, Cal., after criticizing Elvis. This 15-year-old daughter of a Red Cross official was bludgeoned to death with a softball bat in an argument with her foster-brother. The boy told police, "We fought all the time. This time, it was about Elvis. She didn't like him. She didn't think he was any good."

The girl's last sentiments on Presley were scarcely shared by ten Eskimo girls in Point Barrow, Alaska, the northernmost community in the 49th state. Hearing a rumor that Elvis would make an appearance in Fairbanks, the resourceful Eskimos quickly raised $138 for round-trip tickets. The contributions were cheerlessly refunded when the rumor was squelched.

Elvis' reception was cooler in Nova Scotia, where Halifax radio station CJCH banned Presley records as "not up to station standards." Radio station KEY in Portland, Ore., fired a disc jockey for playing Elvis' version of "White Christmas" after the station had banned it as "not in the good taste we ascribe to Christmas music." In Nashville, a disc jockey named "Great" Scott was arrested for disorderly-and-offensive conduct after he burned 600 Presley records in a public park.

Most of these incidents occurred in 1956, the leap year in which Elvis leaped to the top. Since it was also a presidential election year, the two national hysterias—politics and Presley —were bound to overlap. In Lowndes County, Miss., Elvis received a write-in vote for president, making the county totals: Adlai Stevenson, 23; Elvis Presley, 1. President Eisenhower, who overcame the shutout by running strong outside Lowndes County, failed to list Elvis among the entertainers invited to his 1957 inauguration. George Murphy, chairman of the Inaugural Entertainment Committee, explained: "I think that Presley is a Democrat." (The Democratic National Committee didn't demand equal time to deny Murphy's claim.) But undaunted and unvictorious Tennessee Republicans, remembering that hillbilly musician Roy Acuff once came close to winning the governorship, dropped "Elvis for Congress?" hints anyway. These feelers became ingrown when the politicians realized that "candidate" Presley was too young to hold office.

Elvis' ineligibility didn't rule him out as lucrative political hay for those who did hold office. Idaho State Representative Perry Swisher hit the headlines simply by citing Elvis as one reason why no bills that would give 18-year-olds the right to vote had been introduced in the legislature. He said that the affection of American youth for Elvis Presley "demonstrates their lack of maturity. It makes us take a second look at the judgment of teenagers."

While the politicians were judging the teenagers, many religious leaders were judging Presley. "Elvis Presley is morally insane," said the Rev. Carl E. Elgena, pastor of a Baptist church

in Des Moines. "The spirit of Presleyism has taken down all bars and standards. . . . "We're living in a day of jellyfish morality." The National Religious Broadcasters convention in

Washington was told by Harold Fellows, President of the National Association of Radio and Television Broadcasters: "Elvis Presley is one of the biggest problems we've got . . . a problem of American society. Much too many are going crazy about Presley. The better job you do in your field of religion, the sooner Presley will go."

This responsibility was shouldered by a Baptist minister in New Bedford, Mass., when he received an anonymous letter. The Rev. Edward J. Hales read it to his congregation one Sunday:

> Pastor—we are members of a teenage gang. We usually don't have much to do with ministers, but we would like your opinion of Elvis Presley.

Rev. Hales told the churchgoers that he considered Presley an expression of the "subconscious nature of modern youth in a time of turmoil." He continued: "But this is not anything new. We went through the stages of the Charleston, the Big Apple, and the swooning of teenagers over Frank Sinatra. I feel that the emotional nature of young people has produced Elvis Presley. Part of adolescence is change. We are living in a world where it is pretty hard even for adults to remain emotionally stable."

To a priest in "The Pelvis' " home town of Memphis, Elvis was more a cause than an effect. Father Daniel Clement told parishioners of St. Michael's Catholic Church that he deplored Elvis' "suggestive" movements. He advised adults and children to stay away from Presley's movie, *Love Me Tender*, which he termed "at least partially objectionable." The priest added: "Presley's morals may be above reproach, but he must be judged on how he entertains and how that entertainment affects those watching him."

Not far away from Father Clement's pulpit, the most irritating effects of Presleyism were dramatized when Elvis took a 19-year-old Memphis beauty queen, Barbara Ann Hearn, to watch a newsreel of himself. They were, as a routine matter,

mobbed outside the theater. While they were inside, girl fans
scrawled love messages in lipstick all over Elvis' white Cadillac.
They also ripped up the car's upholstery.

In Las Vegas, where minors could not be admitted to Presley's night club show because of liquor laws, frustrated teenagers dissipated their energy by wrecking a ladies' room.

Across thousands of miles and an ocean, hundreds of British
"Teddy Boys" rioted at a London theater where an Elvis Presley movie was showing. They ripped out seats and hurled them
at the screen, slashed seat covers with razors and tossed the
stuffing in the air. Boys in ducktails and Edwardian suits
leaped onstage, chanting in time to the music. The movie was
stopped and police with dogs ejected dozens of boys and
girls before the showing resumed.

But Elvis was primarily America's juvenile-delinquency
problem. Police chiefs and juvenile-court judges made constant,
well-publicized reference to him. In San Diego, Jacksonville,
and Louisville, among other cities, officials banned or modified
his act, despite Elvis' plaintive whine: "How in the pea-pickin'
world can I help it if I go wi-uld when I sing?"

In Bridgeport, Conn., five teenage boys were arrested on
robbery charges. They said they stole to finance a trip to an Elvis Presley show in New York. Said Prosecutor Daniel J. Cremen, Jr.: "Elvis Presley is an inspiration for low IQ hood-
lums and ought to be entertaining in the State Reformatory."

Statements like Cremen's prompted an interviewer to ask Elvis if he thought he contributed to juvenile delinquency. The
reply was:

"If I thought that was true, sir, I would quit and go back to
driving a truck. I wouldn't do anything to hurt anybody, sir.
Money doesn't mean anything to me. It's this business I love."

Driving a truck had been Elvis' only aspiration before he
and "this business" fell in love.

"Ah used to see them drivers with their shirts off, handker-
chiefs around their neck, a little cap on their head. They looked

"How in the pea-pickin' world can I help it if
I go wi-uld when I sing?"

darin' to me. Ah always dreamed of bein' a real wild truck
driver," he recalled.

It was a moderately ambitious dream for an "only child"
who was born January 8, 1935, in a home-made shanty in Tupelo, Miss., a town of 11,000 where his father, Vernon Presley,
was a farmer. Elvis' twin, Jesse Garon, died at birth.

In a family where music was simply a form of recreation nobody could conceive of making a living as a singer.

Elvis gave several versions of his musical genesis. One was
that when he won prize money at a county fair, his mother,
Gladys Presley, bought him a guitar instead of a bike. Another
was: "Mah pah gave me a guitar and Ah became a singah."

More often, he claimed that he acquired his singing style
with his religion. His family belonged to the First Assembly of
God, a fundamentalist sect. "We used to go to these religious
singin's all the time. There were these singahs, puffectly fine

singahs, but nobody responded to 'em. Then there was the preachers and they cut up all over the place, jumpin' on the pianah, movin' every which way. The audience liked 'em. Ah guess Ah learned from them."

When Elvis was fourteen, the family moved to Memphis, where Vernon Presley walked the snowy streets that winter looking for work. The Presleys lived in a one-room apartment in a public housing project. Elvis Presley stood in line Christmas Eve with other needy children at the annual Memphis *Press-Scimitar* Goodfellows party. His guitar commuted back and forth between the housing project and the pawnshop, where it could raise $3 when needed. Big money? That was the $10 Elvis got for selling a pint of his blood to the Baptist Hospital. Eventually, Vernon Presley found a job in a paint factory, where he worked until his son "retired" him at 39.

At the age of 16, Elvis Presley could be found mowing lawns in Memphis at $1-a-lawn. Later, he was a $14-a-week theater usher. At 19, he had attained his goal in life. He was driving a truck for $35 a week.

One lazy, uneventful afternoon, at the peak of his truck-driving career, Presley parked his vehicle outside a Memphis record shop and darted in to make an amateur recording of "My Happiness" and "That's When Your Heartaches Began" for his mother. To himself, Elvis sounded "like somebody beatin' on a bucket lid," but a man in the store overheard the session and said he might give the youth a call. He did, several months later. The man was Sam Phillips, owner of a small record company and an all-girl radio station. When Phillips' operation expanded, Elvis became a full-time entertainer. One of his records sold 7,000 copies in the Memphis area.

He was still just a regional phenomenon when "Colonel" Tom Parker caught a matinée in Texarkana, Texas. The title of "Colonel" was an honorary souvenir of his friendships with the governors of Louisiana and Tennessee. Parker, a rotund pipe-smoking West Virginian of 49, was a veteran of sideshows, peepshows, boat-shows, carnivals, and one-night stands. As a pitchman, he had once operated "The Great Parker Pony Circus" and been a partner in the Hadacol patent-medicine fad.

At the matinée in Texarkana, Parker watched this sideburned smoky-eyed boy sing and twitch and slap a guitar like a bongo drum. The audience couldn't discern the lyrics, but it understood what the boy was singing about. Adults squirmed nervously and youngsters began to pound the backs of seats. Then the girls started to scream.

Parker bought Presley's contract in May, 1955, and became his business manager. "My friends kept asking me: 'Who is Parsley?' We started playing some of the smaller houses around the Gulf. At first, things were sorta lean. But at the start of 1956, business picked up. People were beginning to hear about the kid. The box office proved it."

Elvis landed a job with a Columbia Broadcasting System radio show and then an RCA-Victor recording contract. His first Victor record, "Heartbreak Hotel," sold a million-and-a-half copies. His records sold at a pace of 8,000,000 during the next six months. He signed a movie contract for $250,000 a film, plus 50 per cent of the profits. Guest shots on television boosted the Elvis hysteria to a higher level than that endured by Frank Sinatra, Johnnie Ray, or any of Elvis' predecessors.

By early 1957, the boy from the Cotton Country was receiving 10,000 fan letters a week—including at least 2,000 proposals of marriage.

George Barker, of the Nashville Tennessean, wrote quite aptly that Presley and Parker "took the pelvis out of anatomy books and splashed it across a million TV sets . . . filled jukeboxes and caused family conferences . . . and aroused the greatest passion for sideburns since Rudolph Valentino."

"Colonel" Parker told the Nashville newsman: "When I found Elvis, the boy had nothing but a million dollars' worth of talent. Now he has a million dollars."

But the manager added: "Don't let anyone tell you I made the boy what he is. The kids are the ones who made Elvis. Without them, he'd still be driving a truck."

At the end of 1957, the former $35-a-week-trucker was a $20,-
000,000-a-year industry, although he personally earned a paltry
$1,000,000 of that sum. He became known as "Fort Knox
with sideburns." In addition to income from personal appearances, records, and movies, money was rolling in from Elvis
Presley lipstick ("Hound Dog Orange" or "Tutti Fruitti Red"),
Elvis Presley make-up kits, Elvis Presley loafer shoes, Elvis
Presley leather jackets, sweaters, T-shirts, charm bracelets
(with a hound dog, a guitar, and a crushed heart), statuettes,
pencils, songbooks, photo albums, haberdashery, and other as-
sorted novelties.

He owned four new Cadillacs (canary-yellow, white, pink,
and blue, at one particular time; purple at another; later all
white), dozens of Teddy bears (an old hobby), a live Austra-
lian wallaby, a pair of burros, two monkeys named Jayhue and
Jimboe, a three-wheeled Messerschmidt, thirty sport coats and
forty sport shirts ("His clothes have to be seen in compatible
color to be believed"), a swimming pool, and a $100,000 man-
sion that glowed blue-and-gold in the dark. At a press conference, his right hand was adorned by a ring with four black
star sapphires swimming in a pool of small diamonds. On his
left hand was a horseshoe ring with fourteen diamonds and a
horsehead. On his wrist was a watch in which each hour was
symbolized by a diamond.

Atop a glittering world, Elvis Presley was still sensitive to
the dull thumps from below. Charges of vulgarity and contribu-
ting to the delinquency of minors might have meant publicity,
but they offended Presley's religious and family values. Elvis
asked his mother, the bulky Mrs. Gladys Presley, about the
criticism that was so frequently leveled at him. He reported
their conversation to Associated Press feature-writer Saul Pett:

" 'Momma,' Ah said, 'Momma, you think Ah'm vulgah on
the stage?'

" 'Son,' she said, 'You're not vulgah, but you're puttin' too
much into your singin'. Keep that up and you won't live to be
thirty.'

"Momma, you think Ah'm vulgah?"
"Son, you're not vulgah, but you're puttin' too much into your singin'."

" 'Momma,' Ah said, 'Ah cain't help it. Ah just have to jump around when Ah sing.' "

Then Elvis turned to Pett and added: "But it ain't vulgah. It's just the way Ah feel. And Ah don't feel sexy when Ah'm singin'. If that was true, Ah'd be in some kinda institution as some kinda sex maniac."

The attacks continued. A 17-year-old high-school girl informed her local newspaper that Elvis was "obscene, demoralizing, sickening. He flaunts sex right in your face as a sensual, animal-like thing, never once implying the beauty and loveliness of such a sacred thing." Her knowledgeable letter was countered by this "defense" from a college co-ed: "He's just like a paperback book. Real sexy pictures on the cover. Only when you get inside, it's just a good story." Elvis' respectability wasn't bolstered by polls of teenage girls, who gave these reasons, among others, for admiring him: "He looks so mean . . ." "He's fascinating—like a snake . . ." "The hottest bedroom eyes ever."

Rumors followed Elvis as persistently as hound dogs. "I hear he peddles dope," a teenage girl told an interviewer, who promptly sought a denial from Elvis. "Colonel" Parker replied for his protégé: "That boy don't need a stimulant. He needs soothin' syrup." Other reports that were denied included, "He's been in-and-outa jail," "He's gonna die of cancer in six months," and an exposé in Confidential that discussed his autographing technique. But Elvis insisted, in an interview with a New York Herald Tribune reporter, that he never autographed brassières or their surroundings: "I've written on arms, legs, ankles, any place decent where people can take soap and wash it off. I don't want no daddy with a shotgun after me."

Although an unidentified man in Lubbock, Texas, gave Elvis a right to the nose and then fled in a waiting car, Presley had less trouble from the "daddies" than from their daughters. So many girls turned up in Memphis just to run their fingers through his sideburns that Elvis finally had to recruit a couple of his proud uncles as uniformed gatekeepers at his mansion. On the road, however, Presley was less protected. If he rode a bus, an autograph-seeker would throw a rock through a window in a try for togetherness. In Texas, several stitches had to be taken when an exuberant rake-waver plowed Presley's arm. In Charlotte, N.C., admirers reduced their idol to his britches before he could be rescued by police. After a near-massacre in Austin, Texas, Presley returned safely to his hotel room only to find that a girl had broken in and was shining his shoes. She announced that she was then and forever his slave.

Even on the stage, Presley never could be alone in the spotlight. In Washington, a girl, carrying a baby in one arm, reached out with the other and tugged at Elvis' collar. "You must come home with me! You must come home with me!" she implored. "Just touch me, honey, and I'll frame the spot in gold!" screamed another. Some girls traveled the Elvis circuit, from performance to performance. One who strong-armed her way to an Elvis kiss in Washington left the embrace with a complaint "I don't know what's happened to him, but he was kissing a lot better in Winston-Salem." Elvis confirmed that he was all puckered out. "Man," he said, "I'm weary of being pawed."

Riots were so much a part of the Presley repertoire that an evening with Elvis was banned by the city council of Verdun, Quebec—not because of the nature of his act, but because "we just haven't got enough police to handle the crowd."

Sometimes, the trouble was of Elvis' own making. When the *News & Courier* sent a girl interviewer to welcome him to Charleston, S.C., Presley bit her on the hand. "I was only being friendly like a little puppy dog," he explained. "If you want to get ahead, you gotta be different."

There were other occupational hazards of being a celebrity. A battery of photographers followed Elvis into a Memphis restaurant one day and asked him to pose. Elvis obliged by sitting down with a bewildered but unbewitched 20-year-old girl, Robbie Moore, who worked for the telephone company. He put his head on Robbie's shoulder and wolfed her hamburger. Amidst popping flash bulbs, she protested that Elvis was a "total stranger" and that she didn't particularly like him anyway.

Robbie liked him even less several months later when a fan magazine published a photo of Elvis' hoedown hairdo resting affectionately on her shoulder. She visited a lawyer, who notified Presley that Robbie was suing him to the tune of $42,500 for invasion of privacy. Elvis settled out of court for a harmonious $5,500 "to keep down undesirable publicity."

The settlement did not repel the invasion of Robbie's privacy. One woman called her twelve times in one day to deliver the same basic message: "I think this is the lousiest, dirtiest trick." Another woman asked: "How can you take money from someone as great as Elvis?" But a Robbie Moore Fan Club was formed at Stanford University in California.

Robbie's case was possibly the most orderly conflict in Elvis' public relations. Once, at a Memphis gas station, Elvis was so besieged by autograph hunters that he was unable to obey the manager's command: "I said to move on!" When the manager tried to restore order by slapping Elvis on the back of the head and pointing a knife, Elvis went over him as methodically as a windshield wiper.

When the manager appeared in court, he wore adhesive tape covering a half-inch gash on his swollen face. Dark glasses hid an eye that was almost shut. He denied using a knife ("just one of his hound dog lies"), but he was fined $25. The judge dropped assault-and-battery and disorderly-conduct charges against Elvis. As a courtroom crowd of 207 females cheered, the judge declared unconvincingly: "This is not a show. It is a courtroom."

A month later, Elvis was in a Toledo hotel bar when an unemployed 19-year-old sheet-metal worker walked up to him and said: "You—my wife carries a picture of you in her wallet, but she doesn't carry one of me. Step outside!" Without waiting for Presley's answer, the young husband aimed a punch that didn't land. Presley—who stands 6-feet-1 and sometimes travels with a sparring partner—fired off a few jabs that *did* land. The husband was fined $10 for disorderly conduct plus $9.60 in court costs. When he couldn't pay, he was sent to the City Workhouse for seven days.

The next round of Elvis' fighting career occurred in Memphis. On a midtown street, in March, 1957, a Marine Corps private walked up to Presley and said: "You bumped into my wife when she was walking out of a restaurant two months ago. She told me all about it. I want to get it straightened out right now." When Presley edged away, the Marine stalked him. Elvis pulled a toy gun—a Hollywood prop pistol—from his pocket and pointed it at the Marine, who backed off and later charged that Elvis had threatened him with a deadly weapon. When several days of conflicting public statements came to the attention of the Marine's superiors, they made inquiries. A city judge held a peace conference in his chambers, where the two "combatants" shook hands. The incident was written off, by mutual consent, as a "misunderstanding."

Perhaps because he won so many of his own battles, fighting with Elvis never became the national sport that fighting over Elvis was. From a safe distance, critics, comedians, editorial writers, and educators joined the verbal tussle.

Jack Gould, television critic of the New York *Times*, attacked "The Pelvis" as a likely assignment for a sociologist. Gould wrote:

> Presley has no discernible singing ability. His specialty is rhythm songs that he renders in an undistinguished whine. His phrasing, if it can be called that, consists of the stereotyped variations that go with a beginner's aria in a bathtub.
>
> For the ear, he is an unutterable bore, nothing as talented as Frank Sinatra in the latter's rather hysterical days at the Paramount Theater. Nor does he convey the emotional fury of a Johnnie Ray.

D

From watching Presley, it is wholly evident that his skill lies in another direction. He is a rock-'n'-roll variation on one of the most standard acts in show business: the virtuoso of the hootchy-kootchy.

Most reviewers spoke harshly of Presley. "He represents the nadir in American taste," wrote Eugene Lees, managing editor of *Down Beat.* One critic termed him "a male burlesque queen." Jack O'Brian, in the New York *Journal-American,* said: "Elvis Presley wiggled and wriggled with such abdominal gyrations that burlesque bombshell Georgia Sothern really deserves equal time to reply." NEA Syndicate writer Dick Kleiner described Presley as "libido with a larynx, sex strumming a guitar, desire under the sideburns." A Las Vegas *Sun* columnist, Ralph Pearl, said Elvis performed as though "he's suffering from itchy underwear and hot shoes." John Lardner compared Presley's singing into a microphone to the sound of a "lovesick outboard motor." A succinct review was written by the Education Minister of Mexico, who barred Presley from performing in government-owned establishments because his style "lacks esthetic values and is markedly pornographic." An editorial in the Louisville *Courier-Journal* tried vainly to put Elvis in historical perspective:

> In an age when TV repairmen do not repair, where super means ordinary and economy sizes cost more, we will not object to a singer simply because he cannot sing . . . [but] we don't like to see our kids steamed up by a boy who looks like a candidate for All-American Juvenile Delinquent.

The All-American *Adult* Delinquent, Oscar Levant, added to the uproar: "Elvis makes me feel surgical. I want to cut my throat when I hear him."

Elvis suffered many critical knockdowns and alleged death blows, but he also had his defenders. A Columbus, Ga., *Ledger* editorial still stands as a reply to the *Courier-Journal's* complaint:

On reflection, our editorial for today on Elvis Presley will have to be sympathetic. Being lovers of music, we cannot be a Presley partisan. But . . . we can say that he hasn't had four or five wives, has not been involved in affairs with international tramps, and he's never fired any of his colleagues while on the air.

Fred Sparks, a Scripps-Howard writer, claimed that Elvis "is of the soil itself, like Will Rogers and Carl Sandburg." Sparks praised Presley by comparing him to a fife-and-drum corps. He found Elvis as artless and as noisy, but just as indigenous and entertaining. "I am bored to illness by the eggheads, long-hairs, teacup tipplers, self-appointed moralists, and arty snobs who are running around this country saying 'Elvis Presley must go . . .' " Sparks' fan mail ran 25 to 1 in Elvis' favor, although a Pennsylvania college student wrote him: "I have just read your nauseating appraisal . . . Elvis is a bigger menace to the United States than Khrushchev and opium-smoking."

Repeated pronouncements that Elvis can't sing infuriated the music-conscious Don Freeman of the Dallas *Morning News*:

> This criticism apparently does not question his precise rhythm, his broad, vibrant range, his ability to carry a melody. Rather, it is directed at his distinctive inflections—those "whines, croaks, and chokes."

Freeman likened Elvis' inflections ("Hi want yew, Hi ne-e-ed yew, Hi luh-huh-huv- yew-hew") to the "buh-buh-buh-boo" trademark of the early Bing Crosby.

A staunch defense of Presleyism came from singer Burl Ives: "I think Presley's the greatest . . . He has a fine voice and a great deal of talent. And anyone who says he contributes to delinquency is blaming the wrong party. If someone is going to do wrong, he's going to. Presley isn't going to be the make-or-break factor. One kid gets out of line and a million are condemned—often in the name of rock-'n'-roll and Elvis Presley."

Sam Phillips, the Memphis man who "discovered" Elvis, analyzed Presley's style this way: "He sings Negro rhythms with a white voice, which borrows in mood and emphasis from the country style, modified by popular music. It's a blend of all of them." Rock-'n'-roll, under such designations as "race music" and "rhythm-and-blues," was with us long before Elvis Presley dawned. The still-popular "Shake, Rattle 'n' Roll" was first published in the 1920's.

A Hollywood director, evaluating Elvis' talents, reached for supercolossal heavens when he told an interviewer: "Once in a while, someone comes along—an Edison or a Bach—who's been tapped on the shoulder, who's got a great gift. This boy's got it."

That tap on the shoulder came twice to Elvis Presley—the second time from Uncle Sam.

At 11:15 on the chilly night of March 24, 1958, a chartered bus entered Fort Chaffee, Ark., and glided to a halt before a white, picket-fenced building marked "Initial Receiving Point." Fourteen young men in civilian clothes stepped wearily from the bus and into the warm building. Their leader—a familiar face despite the anonymity of his serial number—commented, "I can't see the ground for the flash bulbs" as photographers and three hundred teenage girls milled around.

A uniformed soldier gingerly took a stack of documents from US53310761 and "on behalf of the Commanding General of Fort Chaffee" welcomed the men. Then they were lined up and marched toward a barracks for a few hours' sleep.

As the recruits straggled in a semblance of a double line, a photographer called, "Give us a salute, Elvis!" US53310761, who wasn't sure he could give a proper salute at this stage of his Army career, looked around hesitantly and caught the eye of Captain Arlie Metheny, the new Fort Chaffee information officer. Metheny shook his head. Then, as the group neared the barracks, the officer turned to the teenagers trailing the procession and said: "OK, girls, these barracks are for men only. This is as far as you go." A small cordon of Military Policemen blocked further civilian passage.

All the girls complied obediently, except one who Captain Metheny swears could not have been more than fourteen years old. She glared toughly at the impassive MP. Then, before doing a reluctant about-face, she declared loudly and disgustedly: "Balls!"

4

"I'm No Star at Bedmaking"

"Sir: Isn't it time they let Elvis Presley live? And stopped tarring and feathering him and hanging him? So the boy is drafted. They make a big production out of it as if he had committed a sex offense. If he had been exempted, God knows what they would have done to him. . . . I am not a teenager. I am the mother of a fine son 24 years of age who did his training at Chaffee. I am not a silly old woman in love with Presley. I would do the same for a rat!"

—letter to Commanding General of Fort Chaffee.

Fort Chaffee and the adjacent civilian community, Fort Smith, Ark., had earned their place in history long before US53310761 arrived on the scene. The area had once been the gateway to the Old West. In Fort Smith, many a hopeful convoy of wagons had been equipped for the California Gold Rush of 1849. The roster of famous names once stationed there—and forever invoked by local historians—includes Buffalo Bill, Jefferson Davis, and Confederate General Albert Sidney Johnston.

In March 1958, a new type of fame came to Fort Chaffee. A gold-laden young man had returned from California—via

Memphis—to make Fort Chaffee the gateway to his Army
career. And a flood of what the Army calls "media representa-
tives" swept past the Military Police booth and left Captain
Metheny, the information officer, valiantly fingering the publicity dike.

Metheny—a Latin-looking native of Arkansas—was working
toward a Master's degree in anthropology during his off-duty
hours, so he took an almost scholarly interest in his new assignment. With firm courtesy (a technique mastered during twenty
Army years), Captain Metheny had a photographer ejected
from Elvis' barracks when the cameraman "tried for" an unauthorized candid picture of Elvis sleeping. Pleading that the
Army cannot fight TV wars, the Captain refused a scoop-con-
scious network's request for an Army plane to fly film to Chicago. In a more hospitable function, he helped the seventy
visiting newsmen find accommodations and he set up a press
headquarters with twelve typewriters, a coffee bar, and six
phone booths. Metheny also granted a request by United Press
International for the agency to install wirephoto equipment at
UPI's own expense.

His reward for this thoughtfulness was three "Congressionals." A "Congressional" is not the Medal of Honor, but the
booby trap dreaded by every information officer—a query from
a Congressman to the Pentagon, which relays it to the appropriate scapegoat for immediate action. Captain Metheny's
"Congressionals" all came from Senators. Senator Joseph
Clark of Pennsylvania passed on a letter from a constituent
who complained about the Army's "special preparations for
that mourning moron. I pay $13.50 per week in income tax
and don't appreciate my money being spent on radio, telephone,
and television facilities for such a disgusting affair." Senators
Irving Ives of New York and Charles Potter of Michigan
bucked their mail, too, including one letter proclaiming, "If
this is the use made of tax money, the military budget should
be cut."

Captain Metheny replied instantly that the bills had been

footed by UPI and the Bell Telephone Company, not by the
taxpayers. Dozens of other irate citizens spared the Captain
the turmoil of a "Congressional" by writing directly to Fort
Chaffee. "It is begaing (sic) to make people sic (sic!)," complained a West Kingston, R.I., woman who wanted to know
"if my husband's $14.80-a-month old-age check is gaing for
plush faculties for Prezley." From Hokkaido, Japan, came a
dirtied-up UPI clipping detailing the Chaffee facilities, plus a
note: "Here is what us fighting troops use for toilet paper
here."

Even the press turned on its innocent benefactor. The Long
Beach, Cal., *Press-Telegram* ran an editorial titled "Foolishness
at Fort Chaffee" that read:

> A rubber-legged, hirsute, adenoidal guitar-twanger gets drafted
> into the service and, instead of letting him fade into well-deserved
> obscurity, the Army public-relations officer takes special pains to
> assure full publicity.

Captain Metheny, relaxing in a swivel chair, leaned back
against a wall on which an Army sign ("Telephone Is Not
Secure. Guard Your Speech.") stood at attention next to a more
relaxed dime-store caricature of a head-burying ostrich ("My
Mind Is Made Up. Don't Confuse Me With The Facts.").
"You wouldn't have been able to hear a dozen Elvises singing
in unison," he observed, "if we hadn't co-operated with the
press just the way we did." Captain Metheny, who had met
the press before as information officer in the Little Rock inte-
gration crisis, knew well that there is nothing more brass-shat-
tering than the howl arising when the military inadvertently
"assaults" freedom of the press.

No battle has ever been so well covered by the press as Private Elvis Presley's first Army meal. Two dozen photographers
recorded every maneuver of his knife and fork as he downed a
hearty breakfast of cereal, scrambled eggs with sausage, toast,
and coffee. "Colonel" Parker, Elvis' civilian business manager,

had joined him for breakfast at the reception-station mess hall. Elvis—still wearing the gray-blue plaidlike sport coat, shiny black trousers, pink-and-black socks, and low-cut motorcycle boots in which he had been inducted—obviously enjoyed the meal and the company. "The chow's good," he declared, "but I'd eat anything this morning." The Army had afforded the rookies five hours' sleep before awakening them at 5:30 A.M.

A reporter asked Elvis if he made his bunk so tight that a quarter coin would bounce on it. "I'm no star at bedmaking, but I'll learn," US53310761 replied.

Elvis munched a second piece of toast in slow motion to oblige the cameras. Then an officer stopped the show, explaining that Elvis and the other inductees had to take five hours of aptitude tests.

They were marched from the mess hall past a barracks where "old soldiers" of two or three days' seniority on Presley jeered, "Give us a smile, Elvis!" He flashed a sharp, sickly grin and then stared straight ahead. When Elvis served temporarily as a road guard and ran back to his place once the recruits had passed a crossing, other GI's called, "Boy, you ain't wiggling right." But First Sergeant Francis Johnson murmured: "There goes a nice kid. I bet I don't have much trouble with him."

The most ironic moment of the day came when Elvis was paid $7 to tide him over until payday. Reporters asked him what he'd do with this windfall and he replied: "I don't know. Probably start a loan company."

Lunch was another circus in the mess hall, with cooks trying to bark like hound dogs and greedy photographers begging for "just ten more, Elvis." Finally the ever-present Captain Metheny called a five-minute truce during which the recruits could eat.

Private Benny St. Clair, an inductee from Texarkana, Ark., sat next to Elvis and watched the action with open-mouthed sympathy. "Is it always like this?" he asked his fellow recruit.

Elvis filled his mouth with potatoes and said: "Yep!"

"Doesn't it bother you?" St. Clair inquired.

"No," answered Presley, still demolishing the potatoes. "I figure I better start worryin' when they don't bother me any more."

Late that afternoon, more than a year of haircut hysteria was resolved noisily at a post barber shop. Elvis and fifty-one rookies were marched there for three-minute "specials." Each haircut cost 65 cents out of the man's own pocket. James B. Peterson, a civilian barber employed at Fort Chaffee, peeled one of Elvis' sideburns off with his clippers and then took the other while a barber-shop radio blared "Why Was I Born?" Elvis grinned and announced profoundly, "Hair today and gone tomorrow." Like a juggler, Peterson tossed the sideburns into the air, but he let them drift to the floor. The audience of nearly seventy photographers and reporters watched reverently as Peterson plowed up the back of Private Presley's head with the clippers—and then took off the top.

"How does it feel, Elvis?" a reporter asked.

"It don't feel so much different than it did before, but this is the shortest it's been in eight years." The longest hair on the top of his head was now a modest half-inch and you could see the skin blushing on the back of his neck.

As the hair fell to earth, a man who had been specifically briefed by the Army moved in with a broom and quickly swept Elvis' hair into a bin already containing other men's hair. The integrated hair was then burned, thereby frustrating thousands who had sought the precious locks. The equality of man may have taken a tiny step forward in the twentieth century when even Elvis Presley's debris was treated "like anyone else's."

Despite his apparent calm, Elvis was jittery. He walked out of the barber shop without paying, and Peterson had to call him back. Everybody laughed. Then "Colonel" Parker blocked off the press as Elvis headed for a phone booth. "I think he's entitled to talk to his mother alone," Parker intoned.

Millions of men who recall with horror their first Army weeks as a bleak, seemingly endless ordeal of "hurry-up-and-wait" would never recognize the streamlined, 1958-model Personnel Center that processed Elvis Presley. A typical stay at Fort Chaffee's reception station was three duty days. One man out of every thirty-five was kept an extra day—for kitchen-police duty. But the odds were with US53310761. He stayed the minimum time.

On his second full day at Chaffee, Elvis was interviewed by a classification clerk and then issued 75 pounds of uniforms and other military gear. Although Elvis was in better physical condition than most rookies, his loaded duffel bag didn't feel exactly like a lightweight guitar. "I'm gonna have to lift weights or something before I can lift this bag," Elvis griped cheerfully. During the clothing issue he said, "Thank you, sir," to a pfc., a corporal, and a sergeant. The sergeant remarked, "He'd make a good soldier if they'd just leave him alone," but the conscientious pfc. informed Elvis that one doesn't address enlisted men as "sir." Private Presley was so flustered by the rebuke that when a colonel asked Elvis if his fatigue cap fit properly, he replied with an unadorned "Yes."

It was a well-attended fashion show. General Ralph R. Mace, the post commander, dropped in to look over the spectacle. "Colonel" Parker was there, trying to insert a Southern string tie into the otherwise standard clothing issue. Elvis vetoed his manager. "No, sir. If I wore a string tie in here, I'd have to take the punishment, not you," he declared solemnly. Parker turned to the milling photographers and said: "I wish you boys would stop taking pictures of yourselves."

That afternoon, the Army made a surprise announcement. Contrary to almost everyone's expectations, US53310761 would not be remaining at Fort Chaffee for eight weeks of basic training. Soon after he finished reception-station processing the next day, he would be sent to Fort Hood, Texas. Some recruits with specific aptitudes had been requested by the 2d Armored Division at Fort Hood for basic training and advanced tank instruction, and one of the men who filled the bill was Elvis Presley. Fort Chaffee had mentioned the name as casually as possible to Fort Hood. After a moment of semi-official flinching, Fort Hood had responded smartly that Presley was just another soldier and could be ticketed accordingly.

For Captain Metheny, this was the best news in the world. Elvis Presley, too, whistled a happy tune. "You name it, I been all over Texas," he declared. "I got my start in music down around there."

The morning-paper reporters—pressing for new angles— quickly asked Elvis if he would give the Texas girls a whirl. The reply was worthy of Henry Aldrich. Said Elvis: "I suppose it's the natural thing when a fella goes to a strange place to try to find a girl friend."

By the time a uniformed Elvis was receiving tetanus, typhoid, and Asian flu shots on his third and final full day at Chaffee, the Army had come to a realization that it didn't have a Dick Contino, or even a *Beetle Bailey*, on its hands. General Mace held a press conference and declared: "I believe Presley should make a tremendous success of his Army operation. At least in my opinion, he has conducted himself in a marvelous manner."

Master Sergeant Johnson, Elvis' first sergeant for his stay at Chaffee, said he had been given "no trouble at all" by Private Presley. He could not say the same for the press or for the public, which had phoned him about two hundred times a day.

While Presley was waiting to ship out, he was grabbed for a detail—"just like any other man," Sergeant Johnson hastened to emphasize—and assigned to the supply room. "We couldn't put him out cutting grass," the tall First Sergeant explained. "Too many people hanging around watching for him. While he was waiting around, he got into a volleyball game with the other soldiers and you should have heard the people swooning and screaming whenever he so much as moved his hips!"

The Sergeant concluded his dissertation on Presley with this tribute: "I don't particularly care for his music, but I wouldn't mind being first sergeant of a company of his caliber of men."

Colonel Edwin M. Connell, head of the Fort Chaffee Personnel Center (a cradle-to-grave sort of command that consists of a reception station and a separation point, where men are returned to civilian life), expressed his awe: "I never expected this! He turned out to be an honest forthright young man. My impression of him certainly changed as soon as he got here. He put up with a lot of stuff that I wouldn't have taken. He's leaving us with a good wholesome feeling."

But Colonel Connell had Presley problems on the home front. When his daughter learned that her idol actually had been taken into the Army, her first reaction to this nightmare was an accusing, "Daddy, you didn't have anything to do with *that*, did you?"

The next reaction was a demand for an autograph, a personal interview, a dinner invitation, anything and everything. Colonel Connell explained the "treat him like anybody else" line patiently and with apparent success.

"I thought it was successful," the Colonel added ruefully,

"until the papers came out with a picture of Sergeant Johnson's 12-year-old daughter posing with Elvis. I got the silent treatment at home after that."

Elvis Presley's last words at Fort Chaffee were spoken to the persistent photographers. "I'm gonna miss you guys," he said with sardonic cheer as he boarded a bus for the 425-mile trip to Fort Hood.

His banter was not to be the Last Word on his visit to Chaffee. A zealous information specialist tried to capture with words the scene of desolation as Fort Chaffee picked up the pieces of everyday, peacetime Army life after another glorious chapter in its history had been written. His epilogue—officially known as Fort Chaffee Press Release 176—began:

> Fort Chaffee, Ark., 28 March—Captain Arlie Metheny, Fort Chaffee PIO, sank away in a chair in the silent press headquarters. . . .

Before sinking away himself, the inspired specialist completed Press Release 176 with a review of Chaffee's role in Operation Elvis. Then he advanced triumphantly to Press Release 177, an imposing arsenal of guided metaphors:

> The Army refereed the three-day main event when nearly seventy newsmen, photographers, and cameramen met Pvt. Elvis Presley at Fort Chaffee, Ark. The tangle of newsmen and the Army was a triumph in public relations!

Captain Metheny lapsed out of his coma long enough to initial both releases and to add a footnote that Life had departed only after shooting twelve hundred photos—a new record for Fort Chaffee; Standing Operating Procedure for Life.

5

"Loose as a Noodle, Flexible as Flax"

"Elvis, we are sending you
Loads of good wishes for the
Very best of luck while you're
In the Army
Serving our country."

—patriotic greeting card, circa 1958.

In Texas, Marjorie Schulten was getting ready for her first "date" with Elvis. It would be unlike any other Boy-Meets-Girl chapter in the annals of Americana. No dainty rustle of crinoline, no anxious dabbing of perfume, no consultations with an impassive mirror marked her preparations. Nor was there any last minute change of clothes, for Marjorie Schulten wore the tailored uniform of the Women's Army Corps.

The silver ornaments on both her shoulders told anybody who met her that Marjorie Schulten was a lieutenant colonel, which is the second highest rank in her military organization. She was a tall, black-haired, hollow-eyed woman who radiated an intensity that had not been neutralized by more than a decade in uniform.

As Fort Hood information officer, Marjorie Schulten knew that she and Elvis Presley would be going steady for several months no matter how well they liked each other. While she waited, aspiring chaperones from dozens of newspapers peppered her with questions about herself, the Army, and Elvis.

Only two days earlier, Elvis Presley had entered Marjorie Schulten's life. The Fort Hood commanding general, Maj. Gen. W.S. Biddle, had summoned her to his office. "I have information that would be of interest to you," was all he would divulge over the phone.

Colonel Schulten had donned her grayish bonnet and moved out smartly in a combat-ready manner. Along the way to General Biddle's office, she had met an anxious brigadier general who had received the same summons.

Major General Biddle crisply greeted both officers and told them, "I have just received information that, in about two days, we are going to receive a famous trainee, Private Elvis Presley."

Like a helpless *This Is Your Life* victim, Colonel Schulten saw her whole military career pass in review before her. Was this the ironic climax of years of hard soldiering? Had her Army advancement led only to this? Was a woman who had proved herself a leader-of-men destined to be the sitter for a million-dollar baby?

Steeped in the jargon of the men around her, she described her unique emotional experience this way:

"I've always played it by ear, stayed loose as a noodle, flexible as flax, however you wish to describe it. But I couldn't this time.

"There was a moment of stunned silence. I'll remember that if I live to be a thousand years old. We recognized it—any information officer would recognize it—as an atomic bomb that had been dropped in our lap.

"General Biddle asked me: 'What do you think?'

"I answered: 'The situation, sir, as I see it, is unprecedented. It will require an unprecedented answer. At the moment, *I have no plans.*' "

Colonel Schulten's admission was a distressing one for her. She noted: "As a woman in a man's Army, I have always looked forward to challenges—a chance to prove my ability. But I didn't know how I could cope with this one."

Neither did her fellow officers, so they held a strategy conference that produced a policy of complete press co-operation. In the ensuing hours, this policy had Colonel Schulten struggling manfully to explain modern Army fundamentals to newsmen whose archaic military thinking obviously had crystallized in World War II or even earlier. "Generally," Colonel Schulten conceded, "the media were not particularly well-informed."

When Colonel Schulten saw that Elvis' imminent arrival was precipitating "a tornado of media interest," she deployed her troops to pursue a defensive action that might still enable the Army to make Elvis a soldier.

"He was due in on the 28th about 4 p.m.," she recalled. "Beginning at 11 a.m., the media people started to come in here. I've never seen so many people. We had cameras coming out of our ears. When I saw a Fort Worth editor with a reputation for never leaving his swivel chair, I knew this was an event."

Presley's manager, "Colonel" Parker, dropped in to offer his services, advice, and moral support. That afternoon, Lieutenant Colonel Schulten turned to "Colonel" Parker and, couching her words in the respect accorded a higher-ranking person—particularly one who made all his rank "on the outside"—she told him:

"Colonel Parker, the 2d Armored Division will not be able to train this boy at the rate these requests are coming in. You have an enormous investment, so you may not like what I'm about to do right here and now."

Parker, whose most detailed pre-induction plans had never an-

E

ticipated a woman officer, gazed at her for a moment and then
surrendered to the inevitable with a meek, "Well, Colonel,
you're the boss now."

That was the easiest part of a difficult task, Colonel Schulten
reported. "I have never felt so much on the brink of battle as
I did at that crucial moment," she said. "I was all by myself,
despite the crowd."

She stood up on a table and summoned the press. From her
unimposing summit, she told them humbly that she appreciated their interest and their needs, but her mission in life right
then was to give at least eight weeks' basic training to Elvis
Presley. As gently as possible, she told them that even today's
streamlined Army had no way to accomplish this in the center
of a continuous mob scene.

"Therefore," she snapped with sudden authority, "you will
have carte blanche, as promised—but just this one day. After
today, nothing!

"If this young man distinguishes himself in any way during
his training, you will get releases, but we are not accustomed to
photographing every move of every trainee."

There was a moment of stunned silence—the same silence
Colonel Schulten had encountered in General Biddle's office
two days earlier.

"Then, seconds later," she recalled, "there was a uniform reaction of understanding—a definite sound that I could hear. I
started to breathe again.

"When other people heard that this poor little old WAC officer had reversed the plans, they were a little shocked, but
they had nowhere to appeal. The decision had to be made at
the moment.

"From then on, my biggest single problem was assuaging
the hearts of the media who didn't make it there the first day."

The press treated the incident kindly and the general tone of
coverage was set by the *Daily Telegram* in nearby Temple,
Texas. The *Telegram* headlined the occasion: PRESLEY OPENS
FOR 8 WEEKS.

The stork delivering the million-dollar baby to Fort Hood was a streamlined red bus that the Army had chartered from a civilian concern. It was driven by a civilian employee of the bus company. Aboard were Elvis, wearing his new green Class-A uniform, a couple of dozen recruits, and Captain J. F. Dowling. The Captain—a handsome, prematurely silver-haired young man who might pass in civilian clothes for Margaret Truman's elegant husband—had been entrusted with the perilous mission of delivering Elvis intact to Fort Hood.

The heroic advance from Arkansas to Texas had begun on a fugitive note when a convoy of unauthorized civilian cars chased the bus at high speed from Fort Chaffee into Oklahoma. Although he was eager to lose this unexpected retinue, Captain Dowling would not let the driver surpass sixty miles an hour.

Passenger Presley, fearing unfavorable publicity, gazed worriedly at the cars. He told Captain Dowling, "I'd hate to see anyone get hurt if we have to stop short. Maybe if I wave to them, they won't follow us and have an accident."

The civilians tailed the bus for almost a hundred miles. Occasionally a carload of gawkers would pass the bus and then pull up short. When the last curiosity-seeker had faded into the Oklahoma dust, Elvis Presley slept for an hour.

Toward noon, Captain Dowling, who was familiar with the local freeway system, glanced out and noticed that the bus was speeding toward Dallas.

Captain Dowling knew the Army had told the bus company to route Elvis' bus directly to Fort Hood, bypassing Dallas.

The Captain approached the driver and instructed him to get back on the bypass route. The driver replied that he had other orders from his superiors. Both men rattled their chains-of-command for a few moments until Captain Dowling insisted that since the Army had chartered the bus, the Army owned it at the moment. Then he clinched the debate by practically declaring martial law on the embattled civilian. The driver gave in, emphasizing that he was capitulating for the good of the Army, Private Presley, and the bus company. Captain Dowling reassured him by sketching the horrors that would have ensued if Elvis had been captured by an overenthusiastic Dallas mob.

The driver assented: "There'd have been a riot!"

He was not the Organization Man he thought he was. The bus company had made a publicity deal with a Dallas radio station to rope off the restaurant in the bus terminal and feed Elvis there. Heavy promotion on the air packed a suffocating mob into the terminal. By noon, just about everyone was there except Elvis Presley. When he failed to appear, a horde of girls boarded every bus that came in. Any man in a uniform had to show his credentials and stand a tense inspection before being allowed off.

Oblivious to the Dallas consternation, the guest of honor was passing through Waxahachie, Texas, where his bus was confronted by a delegation of close to four hundred overheated females. All were screaming at the top of their lungs and covering their ears with trembling hands. Captain Dowling wondered briefly why screaming girls always shelter their own ears. What if Elvis had wanted to say something inspirational to them? They'd have missed it all.

The Army buses usually stop for lunch in Waxahachie. When the mob of girls saw that the Elvis Special was going straight through their home town without stopping, they tugged at their hair, screamed some more, and then piled into cars and gave chase. Eventually, they were left behind.

Captain Dowling decided to feed his charges in Hillsboro, Texas, where they arrived about 1:30 P.M. He scouted a café with a clean exterior and an appetizing menu. The Captain asked the manager if he accepted Government meal tickets and, without mentioning names, inquired if he would feed a busload of hungry soldiers. Only when he had received a reply of "Sure" did Captain Dowling give the "Abandon Bus!" command. But his leadership responsibilities didn't end there, as his narrative indicates:

"I had Elvis sit with his face to the wall and I planted my two biggest men next to him—one on his right, one on his left.

"I think we must have set some sort of record. We went twenty-five minutes before anyone recognized him. Then his waitress brought him dessert, looked at him, and said: 'My! Aren't you Elvis Presley?'

"Elvis gulped, but in a second, the whole place knew it. The waitress wanted an autograph, but I asked her to wait a few minutes until he finished eating. She was OK, but some older woman came over and said, 'I'm a taxpayer. I want his autograph now!' Then we had a mob scene on our hands. The town had been deserted when we got there, but by the time we could make our way out, about twenty-five minutes after Elvis had finished his dessert, there were maybe two hundred people in that little restaurant.

"Elvis was very nice about the whole thing. Some of the men ordered meals that exceeded the allowance on the meal ticket, but Elvis said he'd pick up the check for the difference. And before we got him on the bus, he managed to buy cigarettes and candy, which he passed out to the boys. As we left Hillsboro, the girls were fighting over who would keep the chair that Elvis had sat in."

When the bus reached Fort Hood, it was met by another two or three hundred people, who had been waiting for hours at the troop-processing center. But Captain Dowling was ready to brave any mob, for he was armored with three magical words: "We made it!"

Target practice—with Private Elvis Presley as the target—began basic training for US53310761 in the 2d Armored Division at Fort Hood. "Maybe you'd like the bugler to play rock-'n'-roll 'stead of taps," was repeated with the regularity of a cadence count. "Miss your teddy bears, Elvis?" and comparable jeers were about as common as mess-hall meatballs. When the fan magazines got wind of the heckling, they "exposed" it in lumpy prose under lurid titles like "The GI Plot Against Elvis." Worried teenage girls from coast to coast deprived themselves of jukebox money for half an hour to plunk down a quarter apiece and read the frightening news of chowline persecution.

Despite these man-made obstacles, Private Presley quickly proved himself a capable, well-liked, and conscientious trainee. He marched well, treated his uniforms and rifle as fastidiously as he would his gold-leaf suit and guitar, gave snappy salutes, stopped calling noncoms "sir," and seldom complained. When he failed at first to qualify on the pistol range, he volunteered to take extra lessons on his off-duty time. Eventually, he became skilled with the weapon.

Elvis proved equally adept with pots and pans, compartmentalized trays, and other Kitchen Police ammunition. It became necessary, however, to limit his KP opportunities to those of an "inside man." A perfumed crowd of girls had collected on the one occasion when the head cook sent Elvis outside to scrub garbage cans.

Before even a slight case of dishpan hands could set in, Private Elvis Presley was retired from KP. Exemption came when he was awarded his first military honor—the title of Acting Assistant Squad Leader. This impressive post did not involve a pay increase or even a stripe, but it did free Elvis from fatigue duties and grant him some tentative authority.

Elvis' new designation was given appropriate fanfare. "We're all proud of him!" exclaimed Colonel Schulten. "He does everything expected of him in a soldierly way. He is well liked by his associates and his officers. . . . Elvis is an above-average trainee."

Reports of Elvis' achievements received such wide circulation that Colonel Schulten developed a new set of fears. Were her PIO technicians inflating a capable GI into a legendary

Private Presley quickly proved himself a capable, well-liked, and conscientious trainee.

Superman? She breathed a trifle more easily when Elvis, off on a weekend pass, was ticketed for speeding in Fort Worth. (He had been doing seventy-five miles an hour trying to elude a phalanx of girls.)

But Elvis' duty-hour decorum remained excellent and the Army struggled valiantly with the fiction of treating him "like everyone else." When the press reported that an extra postal clerk was staggering beneath three mailbags of letters that came each day to US53310761, a Fort Hood spokesman replied with appropriate imagery: "The Army is leaning over backward to afford Private Presley the same treatment as the others."

In addition to Elvis' fan mail, Fort Hood coped with other Presley correspondence. Bundles of letters to various Army authorities were toted into Colonel Schulten's office, where she used them to gauge public reaction.

"At the outset, this young man had two publics," she observed. "One was the absolutely, utterly dedicated, and the other—well, he was like Roosevelt. They either loved him or they hated him. We'd get one letter with just two red lips imprinted on the envelope, and the next one would be written in gravel.

"We answered each letter personally, whenever there was a return address or the letter was traceable. Sometimes we got replies to our replies. 'I'm surprised that you answered,' a lot of them wrote back. Others wrote again each time they realized a little more what we were trying to do. I think we gained a whole new public for the boy—and respect for the Army."

After Fort Hood reports of Elvis' behavior penetrated official Washington, Selective Service Director Hershey was quoted by a fan magazine as saying: "Presley is the best thing that has happened to the draft in five years!" In fact, Elvis had attained more "respectability" in his few weeks as just another private than he had in many months atop the celebrity heap. As a result, Colonel Schulten was kept busy rejecting requests for Elvis to give benefit performances, make recruiting pitches for other Army agencies, dedicate civic-sponsored teenage clubs, make halftime appearances at football games, and judge beauty contests. When a Florida Congressman asked Uncle Sam to lend Elvis to an Armed Forces Day celebration in De Leon Springs, Colonel Schulten calmly vetoed the idea.

Although Elvis could not come to the public, his public was more than willing to come to him. Fort Hood was an "open" post and, on a peak "sight-seeing" day, as many as eight hundred pilgrims would drive through slowly, hoping to view Elvis in action. They added traffic jams to the Army's problems. As one of Elvis' commanders, Lt. Col. Russell C. Geist, Jr., phrased it in appropriate Army lingo: "Vehicle density within the regimental area has become greater than the streets can absorb!"

Sight-seers may not have seen Private Presley, but many caught a glimpse of his Army destiny. It was no military secret that Elvis' regiment was training a replacement packet for the 3d Armored Division in Germany. For those who still had doubts, the "Einbahnstrasse" signs marking one-way streets in his unit area afforded a good clue.

When fan magazines began hawking "think" pieces—by authors ranging from a retired Army officer to a professional fortune-teller—predicting Elvis' next assignment, the Army issued an official forecast that confirmed the obvious but added a few details: At the end of his eight weeks' basic training, Elvis would be given the standard two-week leave. Then he would report back to Fort Hood for fourteen more weeks—eight weeks of advanced individual training as an armor crewman and six weeks of unit training.

In late September, 1958, he would be shipped to Germany with 1,400 other soldiers.

Germany was alerted!

6

"Good-bye Darling. We Loved You"

"Dear Elvis Presley: I am writing to ask you to save my daughter's life. She threatens to commit suicide if she doesn't bear your child . . ."

—letter from a Shreveport mother.

The weary graduate of basic training hankers for a girl, the taste of home cooking, and a few old friends.

For Elvis Presley, the girl was waiting in a convertible when he embarked on his two-week furlough in late May. A demure Hollywood starlet kept a rendezvous at reveille by meeting him at 6 A.M. just outside Fort Hood.

The miles melted away and, at the end of the drive home, Elvis was met by more girls—a cordon of bobbysoxers who had surrounded his mansion in Memphis.

His mother, obligingly, had stocked up on Elvis' favorite foods—pork chops, apple pie, beans, and potatoes. Although none of these offerings had been absent from his Army diet, Elvis stoked his stomach with the vigor of a son who has been away too long. His mother looked on approvingly, hoping that her boy would regain the twelve pounds he had frittered away in basic training.

His old friends—particularly those from the Memphis press —dropped in real soon. They made themselves at home while Elvis sat around and chewed the fat about his unnerving ordeal. When he said something good, a few of them even jotted it down.

Elvis reminisced about Army chow. "It's pretty good. Anyway, after a hard day, you could eat a rattlesnake."

Was Army pay pretty good, too?

"Every time I go through the pay lines, they all start laughing, but I'm always right there to line up for it."

Did he write letters home?

"No, I've never written a letter in my life." (He thus disclosed a million "forgeries"; his fan letters are answered and signed by secretaries and other management personnel.)

Why didn't he get into something more comfortable, while he was on leave, than the uniform he was wearing?

"Simple. I'm kinda proud of it."

Did the other soldiers really accept him?

"Yes, after they saw I would pull KP, dig ditches, and walk guard without trying to loaf. We get along fine."

How did he like the Army now?

"It's human nature to gripe, but I'm going ahead and doing the best job I can. One thing: the Army teaches boys to think like men."

But Thinking Man 53310761 was on furlough, so he resumed the life that late he led. He again rented the roller-skating rink. He also journeyed briefly to Nashville, where he cut some new recordings. And he bought a new fire-engine-red convertible to brighten his impending return to Army life.

When Elvis Presley reported back to Fort Hood, he was suffering from a hangover that no Sick Call could cure. Elvis had

The weary graduate of basic training hankers for a girl, the taste of home cooking, and a few old friends.

drunk deeply of civilian pleasures—and the taste that lingered did not mix well with Army cuisine and barracks routine. His mother had a way with the turnips that the mess sergeant didn't. And at home he didn't have to mop the center aisle several times a day.

Elvis studied the regulations and learned that a soldier who goes through channels can usually obtain permission to sleep off-post if he has dependents living nearby. "Dependent" ordinarily means a wife or child, but the term also fit Elvis' parents, for whom he was the sole provider. Within a week the elder Presleys were en route to Texas. Elvis had rented a three-bedroom trailer to be parked just outside Fort Hood. After a hard day over a hot tank, he could spend his nights "at home."

But the trailer proved inadequate, so Elvis rented a house in nearby Killeen. A cortege of cars paid homage to this new landmark, while neighbors bemoaned the undue amount of dust raised by passing autos. Elvis' route to-and-from home became so well known that a couple of local girls set up a road-side booth. "PLEASE STOP HERE, ELVIS," their sign implored. For a few weeks, they netted nothing but grins and waves. Finally, Elvis stopped and paid the toll—a brief chat.

But there were other, more mature women in Elvis' life. A blonde Hollywood starlet, twenty-year-old Anita Wood, visited him for a prolonged stay and then provided fodder for a hungry fan magazine:

Really, I saw very little of Elvis in Texas. He hardly ever got off the post . . . sometimes just for five minutes at a time. And we couldn't go anywhere, even on the post, without him being mobbed. Really, those boys were just as bad as the girls are about Elvis. If he went into the PX or to the movies, they would mob him every time. About the only place we could go without a whole lot of people crowding around was one of the Snow Queen ice places at the edge of the post. I'm proud of the way Elvis has done in the Army, though. Being made an acting assistant squad leader and winning those marksmanship medals and everything!

Her interviewer paid her back with this cue: "You mentioned your career before . . ." Anita responded with an equally detailed account of her recent and forthcoming television appearances.

If Anita was proud of her Elvis, the Army was prouder. He had come out third-highest in tank gunnery in his unit. He qualified as a marksman with the carbine and as a sharpshooter with the pistol. Toward the end of his advanced training cycle, he was called upon to take over some instructional duties.

The 2d Armored Division's commanding general, Maj. Gen. W. Paul Johnson, who had never met US53310761 personally, studied the reports from his subordinates and gave this verdict: "He is a good soldier. He can be an asset to any outfit he's in.

"And he was treated like everyone else. I think it encouraged everyone in his outfit to see that millionaires aren't given special treatment. Like any other man I've ever commanded, he worked long days and long hours and worked like hell. What he did on weekends wasn't our business."

While Elvis continued to establish himself as a solid citizen of the Fort Hood community, a cloud of personal tragedy began to form above him. His hefty mother was feeling worse and worse, and her husband and son decided she should return to Memphis to see the family doctor. On Friday evening, August 8, Elvis drove Gladys Presley to the train.

Her ailment was diagnosed as acute hepatitis and she was placed in Memphis' Methodist Hospital. After a few days, the doctors phoned Fort Hood and requested that Elvis be granted an emergency leave. When they told Mrs. Presley that her son was taking the next plane, the ailing mother—who had remained "pure country" despite prosperity and urban living—responded worriedly: "I don't like him to take planes."

Elvis arrived on Tuesday evening, August 12, and was welcomed warmly by his mother, who pushed herself half out of bed and cried, "My son, my son!" At 3 A.M. on Thursday, Mrs.

Presley suffered a heart attack and died. She was forty-two.

Her body was moved to the music room at the Presleys' Graceland mansion. Elvis wanted to hold the funeral there, too, with the estate thrown open to visitors, but "Colonel" Parker said no. "Mama loved my fans. I want them to have a last look at her," Elvis said, but he abided by his manager's wishes. Telegrams of condolence came to Elvis from past and present girl friends and, among thousands of other sympathizers, Marlon Brando, Ricky Nelson, Tennessee Ernie, Cecil B. DeMille, and the governor of Tennessee.

On Friday afternoon, about three thousand mourners stood somberly in the open air as four hundred invited guests crowded into the funeral home to hear the Rev. James E. Hamill eulogize the deceased. Anita Wood sobbed intermittently while a quartet, the Blackwood Brothers, sang "Rock of Ages" and Mrs. Presley's favorite song, "Precious Memories." Vernon Presley moaned, "All we have now are memories," and his son, dressed in a conventional dark suit and tie, sobbed, "Oh, Dad, no, no, no!" Their brief colloquy was gobbled up hungrily by eager reporters.

Sixty-five policemen herded the funeral procession to the cemetery, where Elvis approached hysteria and the press approached new depths of play-by-play reportage. "She was the sunshine of our home," Elvis moaned as reporters scribbled. "Good-bye darling. We loved you. I love you. I love you so much. I lived my whole life just for you." As four friends half-lifted, half-dragged him into a limousine, Elvis still was talking unwittingly for publication. "Oh, God," he said, chokingly but audibly. "Oh, God, everything I have is gone . . ."

The tender relationship between Elvis and his mother was, inevitably, immortalized in a fan magazine obituary:

> The day he came home from the Army with a bruised knee . . . she was ready to go to war with President Eisenhower. "What are they doing with you?" she cried, outraged . . .
>
> Gladys Presley babied her son, and he babied her right back. A relationship so sentimental it might have made other boys flinch

was cherished by Elvis. At 23, he was still his mother's "good little boy" and he proved it a thousand different ways. He bought her a house, all air-conditioned, with jukeboxes and swimming pool and great carved gates. He got her a lounge chair for watching TV and an ivory organ, and gold-framed mirrors into which she, being the least vain of women, seldom looked. He bought her a pink Cadillac, and a puppy and roosters and horses and mules. He threw out new furniture, and bought newer. He couldn't make her wear mink (she was too shy to go out much) but he never stopped looking for ways to please her.

"Every day of their lives, they spoke on the phone. When he was home, she cooked his favorite foods. . . . Every night before he went to sleep, he'd have a peanut butter and mashed banana sandwich, and they'd talk and talk and talk. . . .

On a night last winter, there was a huge snowfall in Memphis. A blanket of white covered everything, and the effect was magic. When Elvis phoned, Gladys tried to describe the scene. He came home a few weeks later and she led him to the icebox. Inside, there was a handful of snow she'd saved for him.

After she died, he remembered this small thing. "The beautiful snow," he murmured . . .

Private Presley had scarcely returned to Fort Hood when Tin Pan Alley paid a commercial tribute to the deceased. A morose ballad, titled "New Angel Tonight," appeared on the market. It was attributed to one "Red River Dave," and annotated: "To be sung reverently, as sacred music." The lyrics bore evidence of the song's ethereal qualities:

There's a new angel tonight
Up in heaven so bright,
The mother of our Rock-'n'-Roll king—
And I know she's watching down
On her boy in Army Brown
In her angel mother's heart remembering—

Once she held him to her breast
While her gentle hands caressed
The little twin that God made so divine—

And she kissed the little man
Now so famous in the land,
The greatest singing star of all time—

She remembers when he
Was a child up-on her knee
She taught him to sing Amazing Grace—
Jesus, lover of my soul
Let the good old gospel roll
For there's none can take a Christian mother's place.

A touring orgy of grief followed Private Elvis Presley south. Girls who had visited Memphis for the funeral proceeded solemnly to Fort Hood, where they said their good-byes to Elvis for the duration. He would soon be leaving for Europe.

Elvis Presley's last four days at Fort Hood were clinically described by Kitty Dolan, a young singer-model, in a widely-read journal called *TV & Movie Screen*. Despite such formidable competition as "How Rick Nelson Makes Love" and "What Her Husband Did To Doris Day," Kitty's article dominated the issue. The title alone is a blockbuster: "I Shared Elvis' Love; When I Flew To His Camp To Visit Elvis, I Soon Found Out That I Was One Girl Among Many. And Do You Know What? I'm Glad It Turned Out That Way."

According to her account, when Kitty walked into the Presley home in Killeen she found the living room full of girls:

Pretty girls all ages, and all of them crying or swallowing hard to keep the tears back . . . One said to me: "If anything happens to Elvis, Heaven help the Army!"

I said, "You are a pretty girl. You are intelligent and bright, you will meet a boy you will love and marry someday, and have your own children and your own life."

She replied, "If anything happens to Elvis, I can't go on living. I know I didn't mean anything to him . . . but he's everything to me. He's all I want—all I have.

"I'm prepared, however, for the day when he gets married to some nice girl. I know the girl he marries will be my friend, too."

F

Kitty also met a woman fan "who might have been Elvis' mother." The woman was suffering from acute remorse because she had once found his wiggling vulgar. Here was a chance to purge herself! She apologized to Elvis: "Now that I understand more about music, and you, I realize that the music just takes over. I used to forbid my teenage daughter, Louise, to play your records." According to Kitty, Elvis squeezed her hand and blinked back tears.

A younger fan had known Elvis' mother and recalled for Kitty a visit to Graceland: "She was such a sweet lady. She said to me, 'This is all my son. What other boy would love his parents so much? I'll take you outside to see my pink Cadillac.' She was cooking Southern baked beans in the oven of that beautiful kitchen, and a ham . . ." As this narrative continued, according to Kitty, "tears came to Elvis' eyes, but he held them back and said, 'Thank you.' "

Kitty Dolan was, apparently, the only character on this soggy canvas who wasn't fighting tears. She was glad to share her treasure and deeply impressed by the "wonderfully beautiful relationship" between Elvis and his fans. At the age of twenty-one, Kitty Dolan knew the meaning of sacrifice.

7

"Soldiers Don't Carry Flowers"

Q: What kind of girl would you like to marry?

A: *Just like the kind of girl that married dear old*
Dad.

—query submitted to Elvis Presley by a reporter
and answered by Elvis' management.

After six months on the "road," Operation Elvis was ready to
face the New York critics.

Private Presley, his hair bleached slightly by a summer in
the Texas sun, stood on the top deck of the Europe-bound
troopship *General Randall* and posed for photographs. Directly below, an Army band played a medley of Presley tunes
that, without Elvis performing them, sounded almost like
marches. On the pier, some two hundred newsmen fought
their way through a frantic crowd. In its midst, an elderly lady
fainted without loosening her grip on a framed photo of Elvis.

The Army, playing the jovial MC, presented a written release stating that "Private Presley showed outstanding leadership traits from the start and a fine attitude toward his service

obligations." Among the performers trotted out at the Brooklyn Port of Embarkation were some Fort Hood basic training classmates, who were now persuaded by the fan magazines to say a few carefully-screened words. One GI declaimed:

> I think I'm talking for all the guys when I say that we learned a lot about people in general when we were lucky enough to have Elvis with us. . . . He gives so much of himself to all the people around him that you just can't help but improve a little through the association. He's a lonely guy, in many ways, and a little afraid of what tomorrow will bring for him and his loved ones. . . .

For an encore, the Army brought on another GI "buddy," who wore a cloak of reverence as he mused aloud:

> Things that would make the average guy mad as a hatter, Elvis just took in stride. . . . In my opinion, you couldn't ask for a nicer guy as a great personality or just as a friend.

These tributes to a 23-year-old "all-time great" were not enough for the elder statesmen from the newspapers, so Elvis Presley underwent a hectic forty-minute press conference just before the *Randall* sailed. He remained cool and soft-spoken as the reporters blitzed him with five or six questions at a time. In his arms were an attaché case and a book, *Poems That Touch The Heart*.

An early question penetrated like a shaft of poetry to Elvis' heart: what would he do if the "Elvis fad" died out?

"Why, I'd just starve to death," was the heartfelt reply.

What did Elvis want most to do while in Europe?

"To get to Paris—and look up Brigitte Bardot."

What type of girl was his ideal?

Elvis smiled rakishly. "Female, sir!" Before eligible applicants could even begin to form a line, he added: "Even if the right girl came along, I wouldn't get married in the service. I think that if I did fall in love while in the Army, the girl would understand and be willing to wait for me."

Then the *Randall* chugged away while reporters phoned their city desks and engineers began splicing press-conference tapes for an RCA-Victor album that was to be released under the title *Elvis Sails.*

The *Randall* was still on the high seas when Brigitte Bardot confessed, for immediate release, her annoyance at Elvis' gangplank remark. When word reached Elvis that the world-famous "Sex Kitten" wasn't going to be courted by any "Hound Dog," he quickly bowed out: "I only made the statement that I admire her and would like to meet her. There's a lot of people I admire and would like to meet."

But the opinions expressed by "B.B." were not necessarily those of European womanhood. The night before the *Randall* docked at Bremerhaven, fifty teenage German girls scaled two high-wire fences and infiltrated Military Police lines. When Elvis arrived, early on the morning of October 1, they gave him a raucous welcome to Germany. Another five hundred girls—less agile or inspired—were waiting outside the gates. As Elvis descended, carrying a loaded duffel bag on his shoulder, they spotted him among fourteen hundred identically-clad GI's.

"Our Rock-'N'-Roll Matador!" several cried. Another impassioned soul proclaimed: "When he sings, gold comes out of his hot throat!" Cooler throats purred, "Look! Look! How handsome he is!"

MP's allowed the crowd to look, but not to touch. The girls however, were hardly content to blow their kisses and shout the German equivalent of "Olé." One Fräulein, armored with determination and a fragrant bouquet, had to be halted by an officer. "No flowers for Presley," he. snapped. "Soldiers don't carry flowers."

To reporters, who had come in a party mood, an Army spokesman announced stiffly: "Despite the fact that Presley is here, this occasion is strictly a military operation."

In order to keep it as military as possible (and to avoid a

riot), the Army backed a troop train right onto the Bremerhaven base and whisked Elvis off to his "permanent station" at
Friedberg, more than two hundred miles away.

Friedberg, a quiet town of eighteen thousand citizens, was
not oblivious to the Presley storm. A shop window displayed
more than a dozen photos of Elvis and, at a tavern in the town,
beer drinkers with jukebox money had their choice of six Presley records.

But the jukebox was idle on the afternoon of October 1, for
anyone with any interest in Elvis was down at the *bahnhof*
waiting for the train to come in. Several hundred youths had
paid a few *pfennigs* apiece to go out on the platform and join
the impromptu reception committee.

The train, however, passed them by. Shrewd military tacti-
cians had routed it nonstop to a siding at the nearby Army
post. The teenagers of Friedberg were left waiting at the gate.

Safe on military soil, Elvis was immediately exposed to three
days of "open house" for the press. Newsmen poured in from
Frankfurt, about twenty miles away, for they had been warned
that the Friedberg post would later be placed off limits. Nobody would be permitted to visit Elvis while he was on duty.

His duty would be driving a jeep.

A jeep? The press wanted to know why Elvis, after intensive
tank training, had been assigned as a jeep jockey. Was it favorit-
ism? Special privilege? Government waste?

"No," the Army replied crisply. "Mobility is essential to
tanks."

Many ex-GI's, remembering lawyers whom the Army had
sent to cooks' school and short-order cooks who had been given
jobs in Intelligence, concluded that Elvis' job and training
were reasonably compatible.

Elvis, certainly, had no complaints. In fact, after a week of
adjusting to his work and his new address, he was ready to re-
vitalize Germany's already prosperous economy. Press reports
announced that he was shopping for a castle!

A medieval mansion would be just about adequate to house

the entourage of almost thirty persons that Elvis had in mind: a battery of stenographers to answer mail, a hard core of advisers and aides, a steady stream of visiting friends, his father and grandmother, who had obtained Army permission to join Elvis abroad. In addition to lodging, the castle might also afford the advantages of a moat, which would help protect Elvis from all but his most intrepid worshipers.

The less devout besieged the Army with a secular lament: Where doth Elvis get off living in such Babylonian splendor?

The Army insisted that it was still soldiering by The Book: "Private Presley is being permitted to live off post under the military sponsoring act . . . What he rents is a private matter as long as he pays his rent and observes local German rental laws."

But the dream of a castle is a hard one for even a rock-'n'-roll king to realize, so Elvis Presley migrated from luxury hotel to luxury hotel before settling on a patrician three-story house on Goethestrasse in Bad Nauheim, a health resort not far from Friedberg.

Any man who contemplates castles in the twentieth century is bound to provoke Marxist manifestoes. Elvis Presley was no exception. An East German newspaper, *Young World*, was quick to note that he had no voice, had only a limited intellect, and was certainly no artist. There was nothing controversial about this. But *Young World* then reached out for international implications:

> Those persons plotting an atomic war are making a fuss about Presley because they know youths dumb enough to become Presley fans are dumb enough to fight in the war . . .

Army Intelligence had long been aware that Elvis detractors behind the Iron Curtain were forcing Russian Presleyviks to operate like early-day Christians. (Presley platters were a black market item among the *stilyagi*, Moscow's zoot-suiters. And a few members of the "jet set," teenage offspring of top Soviet officials, were alleged to be card-carrying Presley partisans. In Leningrad, Elvis records cut on discarded X-ray plates were selling for the equivalent of $12.50 each.) But the Army was scarcely prepared for the discovery that "Elvis" also was a fighting word calculated to infuriate East German party-liners.

In the Communist city of Halle, a hundred policemen had to rescue a beleagured East German soldier from an angry juvenile gang. In describing the incident, *Freiheit*, an "official" newspaper, pointed its finger of blame westward. The gang's ringleader had brought back some Elvis Presley records from West Berlin, *Freiheit* reported. Even more damningly, the treacherous youth's home contained an autographed photo of *Freiheit's* Villain-Of-The-Year. Judging by the Red newspaper's tone, the incorrigible young man would have been slightly more fortunate if he had merely possessed a copy of *Doctor Zhivago*.

Neuses Deutschland, another official Red paper, promptly joined the attack by branding Elvis "A Western Pied Piper of Hamelin" who lured youth away from the more wholesome influences of Lenin and Marx.

The object of this invective remained aloof. But when seven East German boys were jailed for "worshiping Elvis" and for making skin-tight blue jeans their "uniform of the day," Private Presley was driven to verbal intervention. "Man," he informed an interviewer, "those Commies across the border are really squares, wouldn't you say?"

Although Elvis was under attack from the East, a few hep strategists in the U.S. State Department envisioned him as a truly offensive weapon. Why send bulky parcels like *Porgy and Bess* abroad when Elvis was already there? What did Ed Sullivan's smile have that Elvis' wiggle didn't? Before long, the North American Newspaper Alliance was reporting from Bonn that the State Department wanted to fling Elvis into the Cold War. The diplomats, it was said, hoped to use Elvis effectively as a propaganda warrior, if not as a cultural spearhead.

But the Army preferred that Elvis remain where he was. To

oblige the press and the State Department, however, the Army did detach a PIO lieutenant to query the most exalted soldier since MacArthur. The awed lieutenant memoed back tersely: "Feels he is serving Army and own interests by remaining as is."

Elvis' decision was hailed by Army brass. Lt. Gen. Francis W. Farrell trumpeted: "The boy doesn't want to entertain. I think he feels he has an obligation to his country and he wants to pay it like anyone else and get it over with."

Elvis Presley's managerial brass was less enthusiastic. "Elvis is dead driving that jeep," mourned a Presley press agent who was overheard by correspondent Omer Anderson. "It's not enough to keep bringing out new platters. We've got to give his fans Elvis in the flesh, but Elvis has the soldier bug and we can't move him."

Elvis was all patriot. Pressed for a statement, he replied ringingly that he wished to prove himself a good soldier and "stay out of crap games because I have to set an example for my fans."

Each morning, a black Mercedes taxi made a regular call in Bad Nauheim. Private Presley was driven to the Army base, where he drove his platoon sergeant around in a jeep during duty hours. At 5 P.M., unless assigned to some extra duty, the sergeant's chauffeur was chauffeured home in the Mercedes.

But the rigors of his Army life were greater than they seemed.

Elvis Presley had to grab his socks all of forty minutes earlier than the average off-post GI. (If he arose at a more convenient hour, he would run afoul of roadblocks manned by schoolward-bound German youths.) After arriving at camp by 7 A.M., he had to endure the ordeal of "policing up" the company area. ("Pick up everything that don't grow . . . All I wanna see is asses and elbows.")

At 7:40 A.M., he was subjected to drill call, where the first sergeant made "all necessary announcements" and more than a few others. If the first sergeant finished his peroration before eight, his disciples were treated to a physical training session or an inspection for cleanliness. The next hour was reserved for "Motor Stables," a Cavalry phrase for cleaning and maintaining a jeep.

The rest of Elvis' duty day theoretically was devoted to missions involving map reading, scouting, and patrolling. Translated from Armyese, this meant that wherever Elvis' platoon sergeant had to go in the course of a day, Elvis had to drive him.

The sergeant, a cheerful Missourian named Ira Jones, spoke highly of his chauffeur: "He's a good driver. He's had lots of practice. He's had lots of cars."

Sergeant Jones had one reservation about his subordinate. "Sometimes," Jones said, "I get the feeling that he'd rather have some movie starlet sitting beside him." Then Jones added, in all fairness: "But if he does, he hasn't said anything to me about it."

Occasionally, Jones and his faithful servant were separated. Once every few weeks, Elvis had to devote an extra day to jeep maintenance or a four-mile hike. And every Saturday morning, the company commander held an inspection, prior to which Private Presley and the other soldiers devoted their talents and energies to polishing belt buckles, shining up rifle butts, and sanitizing latrines.

Although his soldiering kept Elvis occupied, it disrupted the lives of his fellow GI's. The Army Postal Service handled as many as ten thousand fan letters a week. Mail addressed to "Airman First Class Elvis Presley," "Colonel Presley," "General Presley," just plain "Elvis, U.S. Army," or even "The King of Rock-'N'-Roll, Wherever You Are" was routed to Headquarters Company, 1st Battalion, 32d Armor, 3d Armored Division. Many were marked "Deliver The Letter, The Quicker The Better." Eventually, the Army was happy to surrender the bulk of its burden to a civilian "liaison mission" between Private Presley and his public.

The company clerk was kept busy refusing calls from Australia, Canada, France, England, and Sweden as well as from all over the United States. Even sentry duty, ordinarily a sedentary chore in postwar Germany, became more challenging. Shortly after Elvis appeared on the Friedberg landscape, a 14-year-old girl was spotted wriggling under the main barbed-wire enclosure with all the determination of a concentration camp escapee. In this case, the objective was entry, not exit. At the end of the girl's two hour ordeal-by-crawling, a guard congratulated her and then escorted her out via the main gate.

If the girl had been seeking a forbidden glimpse of her rock-'n'-roll idol doing pots-'n'-pans, even a successful expedition would have been in vain. Pvt. Elvis Presley did not pull KP. Neither did any of his colleagues. Each GI chipped in $4 to $6 a month to pay German mercenaries who performed the mess-hall heroics.

When Elvis' outfit went on maneuvers at Grafenwöhr, a huge training area near the Czechoslovakian border, the Army was faced by problems from within. "My Security was going crazy challenging soldiers who wanted autographs," reported First Sergeant Marvin Fuller. "There were even officers who tried to crash our lines to get to him. One high-ranking man tried to stand me at attention and overrule me when I told him he couldn't visit Presley on duty."

German soldiers, also training at "Graf," learned to shout "Elvis!" whenever his jeep came bouncing by. One day, a large Negro subbed for the regular driver. He was greeted by joyous waves and then astonished double takes.

When Elvis returned from "Graf," he was one of several men awarded a three-day pass for excelling while on maneuvers. As fond as he was of the Army, Elvis could also enjoy his off-duty hours. The world soon learned that one of his favorite forms of recreation was a shapely 17-year-old blonde.

"I've been dating a little German girl from Frankfurt," Elvis whispered into an Armed Forces Network microphone. "She's blonde, has blue eyes . . . and I've seen her about five times already, which is more than any other girl 'round here. . . ."

Coyly, Elvis disclosed that the envy of a million girls was a lively little typist.

"Her English isn't too good yet and every time I go out with her, she brings along her little dictionary. The other day I said something about a puppy. Well, she doesn't know what the word means, so she goes tearing through that little book. Man, it was funny!"

The fan magazines quickly christened the girl "Little Puppy" and some even set tentative dates for her mating. She rapidly became one of the best-known German females since Marlene Dietrich, but she showed no tendency toward matrimony. If there were any doubts, Elvis soon made the relationship clear. "Friend," he told an interviewer, "get this straight! She's a fine girl, a real honey, and I'm proud, real proud, to date her about once a week."

On the six days she rested, she tried modeling. The little blonde was good photo material for the tabloids. When posing, she couldn't help displaying, among her other assets, a new wristwatch—a gift from Elvis. She also issued occasional bulletins on the private's progress with the German language. "Elvis knows only GI German," she reported gloomily. "He says things like '*Auf wiener schnitzel*' for '*Auf Wiedersehen.*'"

But "Little Puppy" didn't have the Elvisian Fields entirely to herself. A formidable adversary was Vera Tschechowa, a Berlin movie starlet who claimed descent from playwright Anton Chekhov and affection for soldier Elvis Presley. Thanks to the latter virtue, her wistful face could soon be found on any German newsstand and even on the cover of an American fan magazine, which predicted that Elvis would marry Vera and become a German citizen.

But being linked, even in fan-magazine fiction, with Elvis Presley is not always a young actress' key to success. Long before she had ever grasped the coattails of Elvis' uniform, Vera Tschechowa had been adored by sixty-five fan clubs of her own. Disillusioned admirers now warned her that Elvis was "cheap," "uncouth," and possibly "a gangster." And a Teutonic version of Emily Post may have dimmed the lights of love by informing Vera that "anyone who attends theater without a necktie is no gentleman."

Gentleman or not, Elvis was scaling the social ladder. At Thanksgiving, 1958, he made Private First Class and entered the three-figure bracket—$100 a month. His position was fortified by a eulogistic PIO release: "We hope nobody complains that Elvis was promoted before other soldiers in his unit, but he really tries hard to be a good soldier and he deserves it."

"I'm proud to have a stripe," acknowledged Pfc. Presley, who celebrated his new station in life by buying a white $7,160 BMW sports car upholstered in white leather. Instead of commuting to the base in a taxi, Elvis now drove himself—

at speeds well below the BMW's potential of 150 miles an hour. Every day in every way, he was proving more and more interesting as an advertisement for the peacetime Army.

But the PIO troops suffered a setback when *Life* took a picture of a fur-capped Elvis, in winter uniform, sitting on a foot locker with a guitar while crooning a rock-'n'-roll lullaby to a dreamy-eyed sergeant. It was a scene that Norman Rockwell would have cherished, but it was hardly the image of barracks camaraderie that the Army sought to convey. The Chief of the U.S. Army's European Public Information Division, at Heidelberg, breathed fire into a military telephone until the 3d Armored Division's information officer submitted an explanation:

> Pic made at Graf . . . during off-duty hours. *Life* wanted pic showing him as former entertainer, now soldier. I suggested to unit PIO to attempt to discourage Presley from agreeing to guitar pic, but not to insist. Presley had no objection to such a pic. I cannot put myself in position of dictating type of off-duty coverage. If I did, press would have legitimate grounds for "press interference." I do and intend to control on-duty activities. I cannot control off-duty activities.

The memo was signed by Captain John Mawn.

Wiser, and infinitely more experienced, Captain Mawn was the same officer who, at Fort Chaffee some two years before, had made the mistake of describing Elvis' future hair styling as "peeled onion."

Captain Mawn had left Fort Chaffee before Elvis Presley had arrived, but the ironies of military mobility deposited him in the 3d Armored Division just in time to welcome his nemesis to Europe. The Captain—a youthful, jovial man who had sprouted a prematurely white mustache—encountered no further haircut shrapnel and Presley personally gave him no flak. But he was beleaguered by press problems that made the peeled-onion episode seem, in retrospect, like salad days. In the months to come, he would have to suffer nobly and smile glassily as he patrolled the murkiest swamps of journalism.

One of Captain Mawn's "favorite people," he insisted ruefully, was a "delightful girl" who had been sent over by a fan magazine to afford devoted readers month-by-month coverage of their hero abroad. Her ability was undeniable. Why, she could take a mimeographed schedule of a typical GI's duty day and transform it into a colorful, almost accurate account of a day in the life of Elvis Presley—complete with quotes, suspense, and touches of on-the-spot realism!

The girl ordinarily asked very little of Captain Mawn. When she requisitioned the use of an Army library for non-classified research, he obtained approval. When she investigated Elvis' diet, Mawn allowed her to grill one mess sergeant.

But this crack foreign correspondent did not see herself as a mere recorder of trivia. When Nikita Khrushchev set a May 27, 1959, deadline that made the Berlin crisis the most serious threat to peace since Korea, she was one of the first to grasp the world implications. "If the 3d Armored Division moves on Berlin May 27 or about that time, I would like to go along and cover Elvis' activities," she wrote to Mawn.

The Captain's reply was a model of diplomacy: "As to the division moving on Berlin or any other place in connection with the May 27 activity," he wrote, "I prefer not to comment because it would be premature. If the division did make a tactical move or operation, the first priority is the mission itself. Press accommodations are made whenever it is deemed practical."

Although she was let down, first by Mawn and eventually by Khrushchev, the plucky girl remained faithful to the cause of journalism. She maintained memo-by-memo contact with Captain Mawn, who did his best to console her even in the bleak hour when she wrote cryptically: "Can you give me any interesting antidotes?"

Mawn's patience seems practically heroic when one considers that he was also monitoring the brainstorms of almost every part-time or full-time "media correspondent" in the

Frankfurt area. On slow days, foreign correspondents no longer fried eggs on the hot pavement or polled the man-in-the-strasse. They simply dreamed up a Presley story and called Captain Mawn for verification.

"What do you have on Presley going to Turkey?" one correspondent would inquire.

"Presley will not go to Turkey," Mawn would answer wearily.

"How do you know for sure?" the correspondent would fire back.

Mawn would shake his head in silent awe. What would the Civilian Mind come up with next?

The deluge of queries never abated. On Election Day, a newsman wanted to know if Elvis had remained a good citizen by casting an absentee ballot. Mawn rejected the question as too personal.

Christmas brought an avalanche of requests for details of Elvis' first holiday season abroad. What would he eat and drink? With what gifts would he surprise his family and friends? What presents did he expect to receive? Mawn relayed Elvis' response: "My grandma makes the menus and cooks the meals. I don't know what she has planned. I've been on a tour of training with my unit and haven't had time to do my shopping, but I intend, as always, to give presents to my employees, friends, and different charities. As for gifts to me, my friends and relatives make their own choice of presents and I'm happy to receive whatever they choose."

In mid-January, 1959, Captain Mawn faced a major crisis when a sleek BMW met an abrupt end and a Frankfurt newspaper printed an unconfirmed report that Elvis had died with his combat boots on. Ambitious obituary writers girded their literary loins for the biggest assignment since Rudolph Valentino's funeral, but Captain Mawn soon assured a troubled world that "Elvis is alive, well, and happy, and was not involved in any accident." For a few hours, however, rumors of

Elvis' death ran as strong as the persistent reports that James Dean is still alive.

Elvis was so healthy, in fact, that two days later he gave blood to the German Red Cross.

Elvis had already given Uncle Sam another kind of transfusion—and it wasn't pint-sized. By pumping some new life into Army public relations, he had demonstrated that an army could travel a long way on its pelvis. True, the Army had played its supporting role well. But if Operation Elvis was shaping up as a triumph, most of the credit had to go to Presley himself. He had rescued the Army from many an ambush—by declining to abandon his jeep for a microphone; by staying out of off-duty trouble; by answering the most unanswerable questions politely; by doing more than could be asked of anyone, without waiting to be asked.

Captain Mawn was cognizant of Presley's role in Operation Elvis: "We couldn't want a better behaved soldier or one who has given a more favorable reflection on the 3d Armored Division."

And there were brand new Presley fans in every echelon. Correspondent Omer Anderson quoted an enthusiastic "U.S. Army senior commander" in Frankfurt:

"He fooled us all. . . . We had our stomach full of these celebrities, singers, and so on, and we figured Presley for just another klieg light eightball. . . . But he's never angled himself into anything easy, and he shows exceptionally good judgment for a kid worth a few million dollars.

"Elvis has made it popular to be a good soldier. It's great for us!"

G

8

"The Trouble with Presley"

"We've got plenty of hillbilly singers and actors of your talent, Elvis, but how many good soldiers do we have now that MacArthur is retired and Eisenhower is in the White House? Since you have done so well in the Army and show so much liking for the military life, why not re-enlist and make it a career?"

—Bill Russell in *The American Weekend*.

On a chilly evening in early Spring, 1959, an American reporter ambled casually through the dim twilight of a Bad Nauheim street. A jaunty lad of twenty-seven (I am now twenty-eight!), his impeccable garb and modest demeanor gave no clues to his destination—Goethestrasse 14. Its celebrated tenant had rejuvenated the aging reporter's aspirations with the promise of an interview.

When the reporter turned left off Schillerstrasse, he saw that he would have no need to ask directions. Before his eyes, a garish convocation of the lunatic fringe was marking the spot as clearly as a burning bush. A caravan of some twenty sojourners had formed a grotesque tableau before the static backdrop of old frame houses. One house—three stories high; red, brown, and white; not drastically different from any of the others—somehow seemed to dominate the landscape. The reporter realized that the house's extra dimension came from its beholders' eyes. To these pilgrims, it was a shrine.

As he edged closer, he observed that the pageant contained dialogue. An ancient gypsy, waving a photo aloft as though she were a torchbearer, proclaimed in German her willingness to marry Elvis, to mother him, or even to abandon her respectability for the role of mistress. A gangling German boy in a cardigan sweater spat impressively and shouted in British-accented English: "He's a damn bloody fool!" A less offensive youth in a similar cardigan kept apologizing for his insensitive friend: "We are not Teddy boys. We come to see his cars. His cars, that is the best of him. The man is terrible." An extravagantly fat Swedish girl brandished a many-paged scrapbook and indicated, in eloquent pantomime, that she would not hesitate to use it if the crowd got rough. Aloud, she informed the crowd that she had ventured many miles just to set heavy foot within singing distance of Elvis. Among the lesser acolytes in this passion play were several pink-cheeked American soldiers, half a dozen seemingly rational German children on bicycles, and a mannish-looking woman whose black costume had only two accessories—black notebook and pencil, no purse.

Surmising, with vague distaste, that The Lady In Black would share her notes if he ever needed them, the reporter sauntered through the throng like a happy heathen. Although the house's front porch was barricaded like a store window along a parade route, a swinging gate provided access to the side entrance.

The gypsy followed the reporter almost to the door. "When you see him," she whispered in surprisingly idiomatic English, "tell him for me that he's a little like Valentino. Tell him to get a good producer."

Elvis Presley's father—a handsome, husky man wearing an expensive but subdued sport shirt—answered the door and shook hands. A short way down the hall, Elvis could be seen leaning dreamily against a staircase. A telephone was cradled in his arm. "He's got a call from the States," Vernon Presley said. "He doesn't have to say much. The gals do all the talking."

Elvis waved to the reporter, whom he had met briefly twice before. The younger Presley wore what has come to be known as an "Elvis costume"—a shiny black cowboy shirt and black toreador-type trousers that fit almost as snugly as a leotard. The reporter hardly noticed the thick shock of hair on Elvis' head, for he was taken off balance by the apparel. He had expected to find the famous soldier lounging in fatigues.

Vernon Presley ushered the visitor into a large living room that was darkened by a barricade between it and the front porch. The room was free of dust, but it was littered with rock-'n'-roll records and a profusion of musical equipment.

"See that 'lectric guitar, the shiny one?" Vernon Presley said. "I gave him that for Christmas. He plays 'round quite a bit with it. Let me take your coat."

When the elder Presley returned, he sat back comfortably in a faded, well-worn chair. "Guess you heard about my wreck," he said. His car had overturned a week earlier while he was driving one of Elvis' young secretaries home from work. "I had a few rib aches, but I think I'm all right now. Hurt for a while, though." He fingered his nose ruefully as he reminisced.

Elvis walked in, treading in his blue suede shoes as though he still wore combat boots. "My daddy's turned hot-rodder," he said, with a familiar smile, as he sat down. "The guys at the base keep kiddin' me 'bout it. They say my daddy's supportin' me as a test driver for Mercedes."

"That was a good car," Vernon Presley said sentimentally, still caressing his nose. "It run good."

"Got a good top, too," Elvis said.

The phone tinkled in the hallway and Vernon Presley rose. "I'll get it," he said.

"Phone goes all the time," Elvis said, looking after his father. "It don't bother me when I sleep, 'cause I'm up on the third floor. But I think my daddy disconnects it after he goes to bed at night."

Vernon Presley returned to inquire about a girl. "She's 'round somewhere," Elvis said with a shrug.

"I'll tell 'em she's taking a bath," Vernon Presley said. He didn't return for a while, but he could be heard answering the phone every few minutes.

"Worse than in the States," Elvis said, shedding his suede shoes. "But I'm used to it. It's been with me for four years now. There's an old saying that the time to worry is when they don't bother you. Guess you've heard that."

He had been in the Army slightly more than a year. Had he wept with joy on March 24, 1959, the anniversary?

"I knew it was here," Elvis noted laconically.

Did he count the days that remained?

"Truthfully yes," he replied, swinging his unshod feet over a soft arm of the chair. "That is, I count the days I been in. I know it's foolish, but I'm looking forward to returning to show business."

He studied his toes before continuing.

"It's not the Army itself that's a bad deal. It's a pretty good deal. But if you have somethin' to do on the outside, you kinda look forward to returning to it. If I had nothin' else to do, I guess I'd stay in the Army. But there's no business like show business."

He scratched his feet and scrutinized the reporter.

"I guess you've heard that, too. But once you get a taste of it, they can't take it away from you."

Did he feel he was wasting valuable time in the Army?

He shook his mane negatively and explained, "There's so much expensive equipment that has to be taken care of. You just don't have time to twiddle your—uh—thumbs."

He removed his hands from his toes and gripped a metal leg of a dismantled music stand.

"I like to stay busy. That's why I like to go on maneuvers. I had a good time playing Aggressor. You don't notice the time."

He looked at his watch. Prodded by another question, he discussed the sergeant he chauffeured.

"Jones is a pretty good old guy. He's completely the opposite of most sergeants you hear about . . . that I'd heard about, anyway. I've never heard him yell at a guy. And the guys would do anything for him, anything."

Elvis poked at his toes with the metal rod, but he gripped it tightly when asked how he thought he was doing in Stateside popularity. Although slight pauses had preceded most of his answers, the delay was prolonged this time.

"I think a lot about it," he finally replied, "but I can't worry about it. I have no control over it whatsoever. I hope it'll be all right. I can't worry."

Did he feel that his performance as a soldier may have won him a whole new adult audience?

"I realize that," he said, and the motion of the metal rod ceased. "That's one thing, well, I'm proud of it. I hope I've changed people's opinions that I was just some guy with sideburns yelling and jumping around. I hope I got the point across that I did do the job and I don't have to take any special privileges and favors or use influence. Not only to the general public, but the boys in the Army. All my life I never liked to lose."

He paused. A look of determination imbued the somewhat bland face with unexpected character. Then his face softened and he picked up where he'd left off.

"Yes, sir, I never liked to lose. I need to show people I can pretty well do what they do—especially boys around my own age. I wouldn't have felt right if I'd got out of hauling what everyone else had to haul. See, I couldn't walk down the street and face the first guy who'd say, 'You didn't do what we did!' "

The telephone rang outside and Vernon Presley could be heard answering: "No, he isn't here. No, I don't know when he'll be back."

Elvis shifted slightly in his chair and apologized for the condition of the living room. The reporter conceded that he had half expected to find Elvis playing The Soldier Prince in a castle of Heidelbergian proportions.

"I can't imagine how that story got started in the States," Elvis mused. "I can't imagine how any of these stories start. People are always checking with me that I'm buying a castle, that I've rented a whole floor of a big hotel for a party for one girl, that my daddy asked me to be quiet. Kee-rud! I'd like to know how those things get started."

The reporter's recent mood of Old Heidelberg evaporated like the plot of an operetta. Elvis plowed on:

"The truth is that I had my family brought over 'cause my daddy didn't want to stay alone. I didn't want him to stay alone so recent after my mother's death. I brought my grandma over, too, and I had to have a house for them to live in. But those stories you hear about a castle, well, I guess people have dreams and then they come out in print. You can see for yourself."

While he was being discussed, Vernon Presley entered and waited until Elvis noticed him. The son stood up respectfully.

"Elvis," the father said, "I'm goin' out directly. I'm gonna ride around a bit." He said good-bye to the reporter.

"Don't take the kinda ride you took last week," Elvis warned, almost paternally.

"Gotta get away from that phone," Vernon Presley replied.

"Don't you worry about the phone," Elvis told his father, but Vernon Presley answered it again on his way out.

The conversation resumed. Was the Army *really* treating Pfc. Presley just like everyone else? This was a question that had been popped at Elvis before, and he fielded it instantly.

"Aw, they don't treat me any which way. They just leave

me alone. Unless something happens, they just leave me." He conceded that one difference did exist between his treatment and the norm. "They never put me out as a road guard . . .

"If they did, I'd get mobbed," he added as matter-of-factly as one might discuss the weather.

"Same here," he continued, pointing toward the invisible front porch. "There's just a few of them out there now, but if I walked down the street, you'd have a mob, maybe a riot. If I went downtown, same thing. I don't go anywhere except maybe to see a movie at the Army casern. Mostly, I stay around the house with my friends, playing the piano or the guitar. Sometimes some guys from the Army, they come by and play their records on my machine. I don't give out many interviews, though. There's just too many requests."

A youthful bald head appeared in the living-room doorway. "I'm here now," said the head. "Yell if you need me. I'll be in the kitchen."

The speaker, who wore civilian clothes, was Elvis' company commander. Elvis explained that he wasn't running an Officer's Mess: "The Captain's a nice guy. He thought you might want to ask him a few things about what I do on duty. That's the easy part. Off duty, that's where I got problems . . .

"I mean, not just the kids. There are people writing to me. They want to know: Why don't I do *this?* Why don't I stop doing *that?* Why don't I do more of *this?* Why don't I do none of *that*—except for *them?* Why don't I sing more ballads?

"Listen, if you could make a million dollars singing rock-'n'-roll, would you sing ballads?"

The underpaid reporter allowed that, for a million dollars, he would sing be-bop in Latin.

"You better believe it!" Elvis assented. "The people who answer my fan mail tell me the kids still want me to sing rock-'n'-roll, so far. When rock-'n'-roll starts to go, I'll try to do something else. If it goes. Another thing, it may be that this Army experience has made me a personality separate from rock-'n'-roll. A separate personality. Some of the letters I've got, well, I've thought about that."

His talk had suddenly acquired a rock-'n'-roll beat and there was, temporarily, no room on the program for questions.

"About this Army experience now, I was worried before I went in. Yeah, worried! I wondered. I was prepared for most anything. But I didn't know how people was gonna take me. I didn't know what to expect. People saying watch-out-for-this, watch-out-for-that, they're gonna do this-and-that . . .

"It turned out completely the opposite from anything. The other boys? I never took any harassing from them. I can't recall an incident where anyone ever gave me a bad time, because they saw I was trying to do my best and everything, same as they were . . . sleeping on the ground when we went on maneuvers, everything. Some guys tell me, 'We were really laying for you. We were hoping you'd be in our outfit.' But they're my buddies now."

He concluded his monologue with a huge yawn. Then he was asked if he had netted anything from the Army besides some new friends.

"Well, I've had a lot of time to think," he said slowly. "About the future. About the past.

"Common sense will tell anybody that there's a difference between the life I was leading and the life I have now. It's completely different. I lived at night. I slept in the daytime. I traveled a lot—all over the United States. All of a sudden, I'm in the military, taking orders, never complaining. Now the other life seems unreal."

But appealing?

"Very appealing! You better believe it! It seems so far away and fantastic. It don't seem like it's me, but it never did."

Did he find the Army more appealing than life in a Memphis housing project?

This drew the longest pause yet. The metal rod, which had been idle for several minutes, clattered to the floor, unnoticed by Presley. He deliberated and then replied:

"I was much, much younger then. What was I? Eighteen years old. I'm twenty-four now. It's hard to compare life then and now. I would say that some of the times I had then—well, I would have been more than glad to lead the life I'm leading in the Army."

A new voice—an abysmally deep one—suddenly groaned, "Why's ev'ybody pickin' on me?"

The voice came from the phonograph, which had been activated by a girl in a fuzzy light blue sweater who had entered the room silently. She curled up in the chair that Vernon Presley had vacated earlier and grinned slyly at the reporter while her hands and head beat time to the music of a non-Elvis rock-'n'-roll record.

This was Elvis' most fervent flame, the villainess of American teenagers' nightmares. She was a small, cuddly blonde with a bobbed hairdo that resembled Elvis' current, unsoldierly coiffure.

"Isn't she somethin'?" Elvis asked proudly, watching her tongue play back and forth along her lips. "She doesn't speak English and I still haven't learned much German," Elvis continued, "but we get on." The girl purred and then focused on the phonograph, which she watched intently with only an occasional glance or a lip-lick at her Elvis. When she left the room several selections later, Elvis Presley's eyes followed her to the door and he crooned, appreciatively, "Mmmmmmmmm!" She had come and gone without uttering a word.

In the lull that followed, Elvis studied a fan magazine just in from the States. As avidly as any fan club member, he thumbed the pages reserved for homage to Elvis. A maudlin article, by a girl he had once dated, was entitled "Why Elvis and I Didn't Marry." Elvis had to laugh.

"Whooo-eee!" he exclaimed. "Know why we didn't marry? Because I didn't ask her to."

He put down the magazine and returned, reluctantly, to the journalism at hand.

"She doesn't speak English—but we get on."

"I'm not telling you what to write," he assured the reporter, "but you might say somewhere that I consider the Army an obligation and I'm trying to make the best of it. I'm also looking forward to when I return."

Had he planned a celebration?

Elvis Presley belched before replying: "You better believe it! Soon as I get back to the States, I'm gonna put all my friends together and just wait and see what happens! It'll be a happy time. It'll be a sad time, because my mother won't be there to see it."

This sentimental note seemed to be part of a finale, for Elvis stood up and shook hands, saying "See you later" repeatedly. The reporter asked if Elvis' once-thick Southern drawl didn't appear to be—uh—Americanized.

"I'm gettin' away from it, I guess," Elvis agreed. "I'm around all these guys in the Army and, before this, I was in California making movies. Maybe you're right. I still like pork chops, but I never eat corn pone."

Pfc. Presley alerted his commanding officer in the kitchen and then departed. Despite the change in personnel, the mood of the living room was unchanged. The topic was still Presley.

"I've learned a lot about public relations from this affair—yes, sir, a great deal. I think my education has benefited from this," the Captain revealed.

The Captain's striking resemblance to Yul Brynner added a bizarre note to an otherwise homespun evening, but he brought the reporter back to earth with a flat recitation of autobiographical details: He was a veteran of thirteen years in the Air Force and Army. He was a husband and father. At home, he liked to piddle around with a guitar.

Operation Elvis had changed the Captain's recreational pattern.

"The trouble with Presley—my only trouble with Presley—has not been with the individual himself, but with people who call me at home trying to get through to him. Some kid in the States decides about four or five P.M. that she wants to call Elvis. She doesn't realize it's six or eight hours later here. So it takes a couple of hours for her to get the call through, and she pulls me—or whoever gets the call—out of bed about two in the morning.

"When he first got here, I'd go home about five in the afternoon, eat dinner, lay down on a divan, and sleep till one A.M. Then I'd get up and make myself a pot of hot coffee, because I'd know that the phone would start ringing in about forty minutes."

What kind of soldier was Pfc. Presley?

The answer was unhesitating: "He's an excellent soldier now."

Since Army superlatives have very little meaning (*excellent*, on the rating sheets and promotion lists, often means *adequate*; a career man who is termed merely *good* may be in jeopardy), the Captain added:

"I mean, he could be an outstanding soldier if people would just leave him alone. The business about treating this individual like any other soldier—I don't care what they say, you can't treat this guy like any other soldier. I mean, he gets his share of dirty details—walking guard, anything that comes up —but we can't put him on any soft detail because then the public would holler 'preferential treatment.'

"You know," the Captain added, after a moment of reflection, "a lot of our people were prepared to dislike him, even though the reports from Fort Hood were good. You never know what you're getting until it comes. Well, we sat back with this *show me* attitude—and he showed us."

Was it possible that the Captain, as an amateur guitarist, had been an Elvis Presley fan even before Fate and the Personnel Office brought the two "musicians" together?

"No. I never heard my first Elvis Presley record until after he got here."

Did the Captain and Pfc. Presley "fraternize" much?

"No, sir. Not at all, really. Sometimes I come by when there's an interview and once he came over to my house for something or other—I remember, it was to pick up a manuscript. Some movie magazine was doing a story on the individual's military training and they sent him the proofs and he asked me to look them over in case there were any inaccurate uses of Army terms. There were! Well, he came by to pick up the corrected material and my daughter was very excited to meet him."

Did the daughter know who outranked whom?

"No, she doesn't know about rank. That is, we never discuss rank. She's picked up some of it from kids. Army kids learn about it soon enough . . ." he said sadly.

The unique Captain, who never sidestepped a question and seldom gave a predictable answer, was then asked discreetly about Elvis' nonregulation hairdo.

"I've noticed that," he replied. "Guess he needs a haircut. It doesn't show under the fatigue cap and I suppose he's letting it get a little out of hand. But there's a commercial photographer over here taking publicity pictures. If I catch Presley with all that hair at inspection, we'll give him a little boot."

On that reassuring note, the Captain stood up and led the reporter into the kitchen, where Elvis, Margit, and some Presley cronies from the States were eating cake. The reporter made small talk with Elvis and discussed cars with Lamar Fike, the overweight pal who had tried to enlist with Elvis. Fike had been exported to remind Elvis what "home folks" were like and to warm up the BMW each morning. He was honored to spend a few minutes a day with an expensive sport car. "She's like a good woman," he crooned. "She's gotta be coaxed."

Shortly before 9:30, Elvis Presley stood up and said he was going to bed. His parting words seemed part of a nightly ritual: "I have to get up in the morning, you know."

When the reporter left, there were only a few people on

Goethestrasse. In the darkness, he could not see who they were, but he heard them talking. After an evening on Presley's tight little island, the reporter was almost relieved to hear someone speaking German.

9

"When Elvis Comes Marching Home Again"

*"In this world there are only two ways of getting on
—either by one's industry or by the imbecility of
others."*

—Jean de La Bruyère (1645-1696)

"Look what a lift the American Army is getting because Elvis Presley joined up," chirped a 19-year-old Londoner as he bade his 22-year-old bride cheerio and set out to give the British Army a helping hand.

In a command performance as Rifleman 23604106, English rock-'n'-roll star Terry Dene knew ruddy well that the peacetime Army would call on him for no blood and hardly any sweat. But when he took a first look at his top sergeant, he burst into tears!

As Dene regained his composure, his comments were reported gleefully in the press:

"I was standing up there with my tin tray, having my bit of food plonked down in front of me like all the others . . . The thought of me in that little bed with fifteen other blokes

106

around . . . I felt real sick . . . It was grim, man, just grim."

Dene was afforded a rather limited view of the service. After less than 48 hours in uniform, he was re-assigned to an Army hospital for mental hygiene. Two months later, he was awarded a medical discharge and returned to the arms of his wife.

Other arms reached out to offer solace. A progressive Anglican Father in a London church followed prayers for a new bishop with this timely postscript: "Let us pray for Terry Dene, a young man who has been very ill . . . Terry Dene represents the sort of thing I want to bring into my church."

But Terry Dene was to have no spare time for church activity, for he was already busy packing crowds into British theaters and singing *Just One More Chance*.

As a classic example of how-not-to-do-it, the case of Rifleman Dene deserves no more than a footnote in modern military history. But as a contrast to the U.S. Army's Operation Elvis, it merits a page of its own.

And Operation Elvis itself rates scrutiny because of the merciless searchlight it turned on Elvis Presley, on the Army, and on the public they serve.

Even his critics would concede that the operation had been an ordeal and a triumph for Elvis Presley.

He had survived the shock of stepping from a world of absolute fantasy into the olive-drab routine of peacetime Army life. He had become a number; he had been assigned to the rear ranks of the supporting cast; he had neatly deposited his "colossal" personality in a foot locker for nearly two years.

As generals and gossip columnists never stopped pointing out, Elvis had resisted all efforts to exploit his fame. He had, in fact, worked hard to preserve the myth that the Selective Service and star systems are compatible.

For the Army, Operation Elvis was a victory snatched from the jaws of defeat.

The prospect of mobilizing Elvis would have intimidated

H

Hannibal. From previous experience with celebrities, the best the modern Army could hope for was an uneasy truce. At its outset, Operation Elvis was a defensive action to preserve the façade of normal military life.

Saving face has become as important to the United States Army in peacetime as it was to the Japanese samurai throughout history. The myth that "career soldiers hope for war because it gives them prestige" may have gone out with K-rations, but one important corollary remains: The Regular Army man in peacetime must fight an uphill battle for status if he is to keep his self-respect.

His principal link with the public is the draftee—the civilian temporarily in uniform. When the draftee happens to be an Elvis Presley, the slightest snafu can mold public opinion. Thus, the Army became determined to safeguard the democratic illusion that US53310761, while in uniform, was "just like anybody else."

For this objective, captains and colonels were hurled into the breach. Thousands of man-hours were expended as determined desk jockeys planned the strategy of Operation Elvis and weary Military Police held back the crowds.

The bare externals were successfully maintained, but nobody could speak of Elvis Presley as a typical GI without winking. When reporters sought military thinking on the foreign ministers conference at Geneva, they didn't go to the Commanding General of 7th Army; they went to Presley. (He informed them that his fellow soldiers were "a little worried," but added, reassuringly, "there's not much sweat.")

But the Army did make a passable soldier out of Elvis Presley, a result few believed could or would be achieved. And in doing so, the career soldiers learned a great deal about the public they serve.

"The gawky, loose-limbed, simple boy from Tupelo, Miss., was a genuine tabula rasa, on which the American populace could keep drawing its portrait, real and imaginary, and keep rubbing it out," wrote a teacher of American Civilization and her psychiatrist husband in *Harper's*, which termed Elvis Presley "a Major Cultural Influence" (the caps are *Harper's*).

It was a plausible attempt to explain how a rustic troubadour could parlay a second-hand guitar and a pair of swivel hips into an annual income that comfortably exceeded the combined incomes of the President of the United States, the Vice-President, the entire Cabinet, and the Supreme Court. (Even after subtracting these amounts from his gross pay, Elvis Presley could still have afforded to hire a dozen Congressmen—provided they didn't tack their relatives onto the payroll.)

But how does this diagnosis explain the Fabians, Kookies, Conway Twittys, and Ricky Nelsons that this Major Cultural Influence spawned? Each imitation Elvis had become a self-supporting industry. Could the rest of the world explain away these phenomena with merely one word, "America!"? Not while there were so many foreign-make Elvises to contend with: in England, Tommy Steele and "veteran" Terry Dene; in Germany, Peter Kraus; in Brazil, Cauby Peixoto; and in the Inscrutable East, Masaaki Hirao and Keijiro Yamashita.

For the celebrity system is universal. Once upon a time, worshipers danced feverishly around primitive idols, offered human sacrifices, and passed along a carefully recorded mythology about various gods. Nowadays, the faithful congregate at dockside to pay homage to an arriving or departing singer, faint or occasionally commit suicide in his honor, and support fan magazines that reveal whether their idol sleeps in the raw and, now and then, with whom.

During the past century, there has been a steady decline in quality among the objects of public fanaticism. There has also been a decline in the mode of appreciation. In the nineteenth century, grown women merely swooned when Franz Liszt sat down to play. But in the 1940's, girls in their midteens assaulted Frank Sinatra with such ferocity that a bodyguard with a pugilistic past, after watching them, was moved

to remark that "boxers fight cleaner." Today, in the Era of
Elvis Presley, no star has truly "arrived" unless he has been
stripped to his shorts at least once by a clamorous mob of juve-
niles.

What sustains the clamor?

In the case of Elvis Presley, it is difficult to say. His conspicu-
ous lack of talent has never been masked. His looks have
been compared to "a Walt Disney goldfish with sideburns."
His personality is bland.

Then wherein lies his appeal?

Partly in that florid smile, partly in those flowing locks.
Partly in the floating hips that were frequently declared "off
limits." And partly, too, in a distinction that Elvis has never
truly appreciated: he has improved on The American Dream!

Work hard, be thrifty, and you shall succeed! Whatsoever a
man soweth, that shall he also reap!

Without working hard, without being thrifty, Elvis Presley
achieved a new peak of eminence. And adults who gaze up
at him can see a modern travesty of the Horatio Alger legend.
Here is a young man who has not worked diligently to achieve
his fame! Here is a hero who spends his winnings on Cadillacs
and girls! Here is a success story that could happen to you and
me! Even those who have lost faith in themselves can at least
find vicarious comfort in the tenderness Elvis has kept for his
parents. The thought that just anybody's son can grow up to
wear a gold-leaf suit may be reason enough for bringing children into this gray world.

If adults are susceptible to an Enchanter, children are even
more so. Thus, the cherry-vanilla and butter-pecan crowd con-
stitutes the hard core of Presleyism. Their spell is maintained
by controversy (Elvis' wiggle must symbolize many a youth's
revolt against revolted parents); by gossip columnists (who
thrive on glittering names and abhor drab facts); and by fan
magazines, an item of Americana that even the "mass culture"
analysts tend to ignore. The slickest of the fan magazines,
Modern Screen, sells more than a million copies a month,

while *Harper's* is trying to clear the 200,000 mark. Both have carried articles on Elvis. *Modern Screen*, apparently, has one advantage: if Elvis comes on page twenty-six, can his imitators be far behind?

Perhaps his imitators provide the most serious argument against Presleyism. Fabian Forte was unearthed at 14 by an astute Philadelphia record entrepreneur who, according to *Time*, "saw in the round-shouldered boy with the smooth olive skin and the sharp ducktail haircut just the sort of all-American appeal he was looking for."

By the time he was 16, Fabian had exhausted the patience of three voice teachers—yet his records were selling! And his personal appearances were garnering up to $12,000 a night. He was even being hailed as an Elvis "with the quality of the boy next door." But he still couldn't sing without electronic magic.

What did it matter? "Singing ability is one of the least essential qualifications for success as a pop singer today," writes John S. Wilson, jazz critic and record reviewer for the New York *Times*. Wilson adds:

> Recording techniques have become so ingenious that almost anyone can seem to be a singer. A small, flat voice can be souped up by emphasizing the low frequencies and piping the result through an echo chamber. A slight speeding up of the recording tape can bring a brighter, happier sound to a naturally drab singer or clean the weariness out of a tired voice. Wrong notes can be snipped out of the tape and replaced by notes taken from other parts of the tape.

Although Elvis Presley's "shake and rattle" are partly the product of an echo chamber, he has always been able to sing passably around the house or in his jeep. Onstage, he takes command and occasionally subdues the din he has evoked. Compared to his rivals, who collectively display no more stage presence than the singing chorus in a burlesque show, Presley stands out like a fig leaf in a trunkful of Bikinis.

Teenage magnetism, no matter how artifically induced, is the power that sustains an Elvis and creates a Fabian. It is the pull that sells fan magazines. It is the force that blights our landscape with drive-ins exhibiting *I Was a Teenage Werewolf, The Cool and the Crazy,* and *Diary of a High School Bride.*

For the teenager is now the well-heeled and over-indulged monarch of the American market place.

Teenage buying power has more than outpaced mid-century inflation. Within the last fifteen years, the teenager's average weekly income has grown from $2.50 to $10.00. Last year, America's eighteen million teenagers spent more than ten billion dollars—a phenomenal portion of it on Elvis and his ilk.

Eugene Gilbert, a consultant on teenage matters, has estimated that, aside from twenty-nine cents spent on lunch and school supplies, a teenager's dollar is free from all claims except the possessor's whims. "Some teenagers," Gilbert writes, "actually have more free money to spend than their parents, who must meet all kinds of fixed obligations, among them the support of the teenagers in question."

The high birth rate that followed World War II insures a population that will soon include thirty-four million teenagers. There will be room at the top for a dozen Elvises. There will be ample space in this Brave New World for disc jockeys, used-car dealers, bubble-gum vendors, ice-cream salesmen, deodorant bottlers, and marriage counselors. Perhaps 1984 will be obsolete by 1970.

As a soldier making the world safe for teenage consumers, Pfc. Elvis Presley was rewarded. In June, 1959, the Army promoted him to the $122-a-month niche of Specialist Fourth Class, the technical and social equivalent of a corporal. Responding to the honor, Elvis spoke out like a true noncom: "I'm doing OK in this man's Army—and take it from me, it's a rough tough Army that could give anybody, anywhere, any time, one hell of a fight."

Almost instantly, Elvis was rendered hors de combat when his celebrated tonsils acted up. But after a week in bed at the Army's 97th General Hospital in Frankfurt, Elvis was returned to duty with tonsils intact. He promptly murmured reassurance in an exclusive telephone interview with New York *Journal-American* reporter James Lee: "It was touch and go whether they'd snatch my cotton-pickin' tonsils, but my fever burned out."

Elvis convalesced on a furlough tour of Europe. He spent two nights making the rounds of Munich's strip-tease palaces. At the Munich Moulin Rouge, an artist named Marianne dedicated a special routine to him. Although she wore nothing but an Elvis Presley long-playing record, aesthetic music-lovers implored Marianne to strip down to a 45-RPM disc.

After Munich, Elvis crossed the Alps for an "incognito invasion" of Paris. The date and hour of his arrival were so skillfully leaked that Elvis made the front page of nearly every Paris newspaper. He was pictured popping champagne corks at the Lido, which, according to the Associated Press, "has so many nude show girls it exports them to Las Vegas."

In the summer of 1959, Elvis Presley shipped his father home to ready the Memphis Cadillacs for his triumphant return. Vernon Presley warned interviewers that a storm of criticism would accompany Elvis' return to public life in 1960. "People are gonna criticize whether you're wearin' wings or an overcoat," the father mused.

But while Elvis wore Army greens, the public made fewer and fewer complaints. It turned its prejudices to other crucial battles—heat vs. humidity; Gibsons vs. Gimlets; big cars vs. bigger cars—and left Elvis Presley to his jeep. Nobody raised a shaggy eyebrow when a recording of *When Elvis Comes Marching Home Again* was announced.

Soldiering above and beyond the call of peacetime duty

won Elvis Presley a badge of respectability that he had been unable to buy as a civilian millionaire. The Army also contributed toward his institutional status in entertainment circles, where a rock-'n'-roll idol's longevity is usually measured in days. By pretending that he was just like anybody else, the Army had demonstrated to the world The Importance Of Being Elvis.

Acknowledgments

While working on *Operation Elvis* I felt strongly indebted to 179,714,579 Americans, without whose antics there would have been very little to write about.

Several of them were mentioned by name in the pages of this book. But many others made equally valuable contributions to my understanding of the events I relate.

Two excellent road maps to the celebrity system were Hortense Powdermaker's anthropological study, *Hollywood: The Dream Factory* (Little, Brown, 1950), and Leo C. Rosten's *Hollywood: The Movie Colony, The Movie Makers* (Harcourt, Brace, 1941). And I might not have made it through the Teenage Jungle without Dwight Macdonald's two-part *New Yorker* profile of Eugene Gilbert, "A Caste, A Culture, A Market" (November 22 and 29, 1958). E.J. Kahn, Jr's, slim study of Frank Sinatra, *The Voice: The Story of An American Phenomenon* (Harper & Brothers, 1947), offered incidental nutrition.

The clinical observations of authoress "lu murphy" (the little letters are her coy literary whim), who took a psychiatrist to an Elvis rally, were valuable to me, although they did not find their way into this book. So were the more detached views of James Poling in *Pageant* and George Riemer in *This Week*. The "Elvis Horoscopes" by Mme. Calliope St. George, "international astrologer" for *Movie Life*, enabled me to realize the cosmic significance of my work.

A paragraph—and, fortunately, no more than that—must be reserved for the mention of copyrighted songs that occur at length in the text. These are "The All-American Boy," by Bill Parsons and Orville Lunsford, and "New Angel Tonight," by Red River Dave. Similar acknowledgment must be made to Ideal Publishing Company for permission to quote from its one-shot fan magazine, *Elvis in The Army*; and to *TV & Movie Screen* for the collected prose of Kitty Dolan.

In the course of my research, I visited Memphis, where one now can buy several different picture postal views of Elvis Presley's mansion. Thanks to my long talks with Milton Bowers, Sr., the man who drafted Elvis, and the co-operation of the *Press-Scimitar's* staff, my glimpse of Presleyland was more distinct than wholesome. I am particularly indebted to City Editor Null Adams and Staff Writer Clark Porteous, as well as to Amusement Editor Edwin Howard and staffers Thomas N. Pappas, Robert Johnson, James H. White, and James F. Page, Jr.

When it comes to thanking Army people, a well-meaning civilian who writes a controversial book can inadvertently place an indelible blot on their records. Therefore, I will say only that Lieutenant Colonel Marjorie Schulten, Captain Arlie Metheny, and Captain John J. Mawn are three of the most human people in the service.

My own colleagues at the Louisville *Courier-Journal* were very understanding, despite the burden imposed on them by my leave-of-absence. Only three, on learning the subject of the book, inquired, "Under what pseudonym are you writing the book?" My executive editor, James S. Pope, Sr., very kindly gave me ample time off for jetting to Europe and DC-3ing around the Southwest. My editor-in-chief, Barry Bingham, visited Germany after I did and volunteered to do some supplementary legwork. The *Courier-Journal's* librarians—and particularly Messrs. Martin Moran and Ralph Shoemaker—were most tolerant of my penchant for checking facts.

"Colonel" Tom Parker; his aide, Tom Diskin; and his protege, Specialist Elvis Presley, all were most co-operative. They made no attempts to interfere with this study or distort my judgments.

My agents, Martha Winston and Emilie Jacobson, worked the magic of transforming an idea into a contract.

And my editor, Robert Lescher, was at least as important to *Operation Elvis* as Specialist Presley was.